PRAYER

An Audience with the King

Joel V. Petermann

NORTHWESTERN PUBLISHING HOUSE
Milwaukee, Wisconsin

All Scripture quotations, unless otherwise indicated, are taken from the HOLY BIBLE, NEW INTERNATIONAL VERSION®. NIV®. Copyright © 1973, 1978, 1984 by International Bible Society. Used by permission of Zondervan Publishing House. All rights reserved.

The "NIV" and "New International Version" trademarks are registered in the United States Patent and Trademark Office by International Bible Society. Use of either trademark requires the permission of International Bible Society.

All rights reserved. No part of this publication may be reproduced, stored in a retrieval system, or transmitted in any form or by any means—electronic, mechanical, photocopying, recording, or otherwise—except for brief quotations in reviews, without prior permission from the publisher.

Library of Congress Control Number : 99-80080
Northwestern Publishing House
1250 N. 113th St., Milwaukee, WI 53226-3284
© 2001 by Northwestern Publishing House
Published 2001
Printed in the United States of America
ISBN 0-8100-1223-5

Table of Contents

Editor's Preface 5

Introduction 7

1. The King—The One to Whom We Pray 11
2. The Subjects—Those Seeking an Audience 17
3. An Audience—The Right to Speak and Be Heard 27
4. The Father-King Speaks First! 41
5. We Speak to the King 53
6. We Bring Our Requests to the King 69
7. Common Courtesy—The Etiquette of Prayer 81
8. More Etiquette: Language and Location 95
9. An Open Invitation from the King 107
10. Our Petitions to Our Father-King 125
11. The Father-King Answers Prayer 137
12. Handbook on Prayer 149

Endnotes 165

For Further Reading 169

Scripture Index 171

Subject Index 177

Editor's Preface

The People's Bible Teachings is a series of books on all of the main doctrinal teachings of the Bible.

Following the pattern set by The People's Bible series, these books are written especially for laypeople. Theological terms, when used, are explained in everyday language so that people can understand them. The authors show how Christian doctrine is drawn directly from clear passages of Scripture and then how those doctrines apply to people's faith and life. Most importantly, these books show how every teaching of Scripture points to Christ, our only Savior.

The authors of The People's Bible Teachings are parish pastors and professors who have had years of experience teaching the Bible. They are men of scholarship and practical insight.

We take this opportunity to express our gratitude to Professor Leroy Dobberstein of Wisconsin Lutheran Seminary, Mequon, Wisconsin, and Professor Thomas Nass of Martin Luther College, New Ulm, Minnesota, for serving as consultants for this series. Their insights and assistance have been invaluable.

We pray that the Lord will use these volumes to help his people grow in their faith, knowledge, and understanding of his saving teachings, which he has revealed to us in the Bible. To God alone be the glory.

Curtis A. Jahn
Series Editor

Introduction

Kings and royal courts are not part of our everyday lives. There once was a time when most people owed allegiance to a king and received protection in return. For most of us, however, those days are past. Yet they are not completely foreign to us. We read books and watch movies about kings and queens and their courts. We read about ancient kingdoms and study their kings in our Bibles.

From what history tells us, the ancient court was an awesome place. Often the king's throne was elevated above everyone else so that there was no question about who was in authority. The king was set apart from his subjects. He was the master of all. He was ruler supreme. Often his throne was located in a grand hall where he was surrounded by servants and advisors, bodyguards and jesters. When someone came to speak to the king, that person did not just waltz in and begin to speak. First he had to be announced. The king had to grant him an audience—if the king so desired.

There is a parallel in our society. Though the president of the United States does not sit on some high and lofty throne, he is still treated with respect. He is still surrounded by bodyguards and advisors. For the most part, he is still kept separate from the rest of the populace. He sits in his Oval Office. There he greets visitors. Can anyone simply "drop by" for a visit? Hardly. Visitors must have an invitation. They must be announced. They must know some senator or member of congress who can gain an audience for them with "Mr. President."

Why all the concern about kings and their courts? Because the context of much of Scripture is the ancient king and his court. Indeed, we are members of a royal family. Repeatedly, Scripture speaks of the kingdom of heaven or the kingdom of God. In the Old Testament, the Bible repeatedly uses the phrase "Sovereign LORD." This expression translates the personal name of God plus another Hebrew word that means "master" or "ruler." It reminds us that there are subjects/servants and there is a ruler/master. Therefore, we are not surprised to find in Psalms, Isaiah, Ezekiel, Daniel, and Revelation descriptions of the Lord seated on a throne—the seat of a king. These descriptions, however, are much less a depiction of an actual place (since the Lord fills the universe) as they are of a relationship—a relationship between people on this earth and God.

Those who believe in Jesus Christ as their Savior from sin are members (subjects) of this kingdom. The kingdom itself actually belongs by right to Jesus Christ, who is called the King of kings. When the angel Gabriel announced the coming birth of the Christ Child, he said, "His kingdom will never end" (Luke 1:33). And Jesus himself replied to Pilate's query "Are you the king of the Jews?" by saying, "My kingdom is not of this world" (John 18:33,36). On another occasion, to a different audience, Jesus further identified his royal ruling activity: "The kingdom of God is within you" (Luke 17:21). The kingdom of Christ is unlike any other. Even entrance into this kingdom is unique. Jesus told Nicodemus, "No one can enter the kingdom of God unless he is born of water and the Spirit" (John 3:5). God wants us to be part of this kingdom. Jesus comforted his disciples by saying, "Do not be afraid, little flock, for your Father has been pleased to give you the kingdom" (Luke 12:32).

If we are to understand prayer as the Bible teaches us to understand prayer, it is helpful to be aware of this king and kingdom theme that permeates Scripture. In prayer we are invited to have an audience with the King. Marvelously, in prayer we have the opportunity to come into the court of heaven and talk to the King of the universe.

The purpose of this book is to study this audience we have with the King. First we will need to understand who the King is. Then we will need to consider what our status is before the King. Then we can consider how and with what words it is proper for us to speak with our King.

It is hoped that this book would help us in our prayers. It is hoped that we may be led to increasingly treasure and use our marvelous audience with the King!

1

The King—The One to Whom We Pray

An awesome King

The one to whom we pray is a King. What images come into your mind when you hear the word *king*? Who are the rulers of the past that form and influence your idea of a king? Do you think of the great pharaohs of Egypt, who in the days of their glory erected the pyramids and the sphinx? Or do you perhaps think of great King David or perhaps his wise son, Solomon? Or do more recent images of royalty cross your mind, such as King Henry VIII of England or one of the great Louises of France? Or are the only real rulers you are acquainted with the men of power from our present age? Do you hear the word *king* and think of the president of the United States or the prime minister of Canada or Great Britain? No matter what starting point you have for your conception of a king, it will fall far short of the King to whom we pray. The King to whom we pray is unlike any earthly king we could envision.

The Lord is an awesome King. As we page through the descriptions that Scripture gives us of the Lord as King, we see first that his lordship is far above any earthly king's. The psalmist celebrates God's lordship when he writes, "Sing praises to God, sing praises; sing praises to our King, sing praises. For God is the King of all the earth; sing to him a psalm of praise" (Psalm 47:6,7). Note that the Scriptures call God "King" and "the King of all the earth." As such, he is worthy of our praise. Similarly, Jeshoshaphat, himself a king in Judah, acknowledged that there is no ruler on earth who compares to the Lord. He prayed, "O LORD, God of our fathers, are you not the God who is in heaven? You rule over all the kingdoms of the nations. Power and might are in your hand, and no one can withstand you" (2 Chronicles 20:6).

The Lord's reign, however, is not limited to earthly domains. The Lord is truly an awesome King because his lordship extends into the heavenly realms. "For the LORD is the great God, the great King above all gods" (Psalm 95:3). The psalmist is not admitting here that there are other gods. He is, however, declaring that no matter what one might call a god, the Lord is greater. His kingship is superior to everything that tries to set itself up as ruler in heaven or on earth. This is ultimately what Paul wanted his dear coworker Timothy to realize when he wrote the following: "God, the blessed and only Ruler, the King of kings and Lord of lords, who alone is immortal and who lives in unapproachable light, whom no one has seen or can see. To him be honor and might forever. Amen" (1 Timothy 6:15,16). Even if a person becomes a king on this earth, he is still not number one. There is only one Number One. That is the Lord. He is the *only* Ruler. This is because all others die. Only one remains the same. Only one is immortal. This One is the Lord. He is an awesome King—so awesome, in fact, that his glory blazes like a blinding light so bright that no mortal can approach him. This is the King to whom we pray.

We usually associate kingship with power. To rule is to have control. To have control takes power. The King to whom we pray is powerful. He has creative power. He is greater than our whole universe. Scripture tells us that he created all things by simply speaking his almighty word. I can say "Let there be a tree!" all I want. Nothing happens. When this King says "Let there be a tree!" a tree immediately exists. In just six days his power created all that we see around us. Nothing he made was flawed in the least bit. How many times haven't you opened a new toy or tool or some other appliance and found a piece missing or something broken or defective? Our "creations" are imperfect. This King's power, however, is perfect: no flaws, no missing pieces, no recalls.

Witness his power in action as the one who created all things also controls them for his own purposes. Recall the power that parted the Red Sea for the people of Israel as they left Egypt (Exodus 14:21,22) and parted the Jordan River when they crossed into the Promised Land (Joshua 3:15-17). Imagine the power that could cause the walls of Jericho to fall down as if they were a child's building blocks (Joshua 6:20). Consider the power that could command a huge fish, a fish large enough to swallow a man, to swallow

Jonah at just the right time to keep him from drowning and then spit him out on the shore where he could drag himself up out of the surf (Jonah 1:17; 2:10). Who of us would flatter himself with entertaining the thought of being able to catch such a huge fish, let alone convincing it to do his bidding? This King could take a few loaves of bread and a meager catch of fish and turn it into a feast for more than five thousand people (Matthew 14:19-21). This King could command the gale force winds of the Sea of Galilee to stop blowing (8:26). This King could bring dead people back to life (9:24,25). This is the power that resides in this King. This is the King to whom we pray.

A just King

There is something else kings do that we ought not to forget. Kings are not only powerful, but they also use their power to carry out justice. So it is with the King of kings as well. He is a just ruler. He does not tolerate insubordination and lawlessness. When he sees such things, he takes action to stop them. So Jeremiah declares, "The LORD is the true God; he is the living God, the eternal King. When he is angry, the earth trembles; the nations cannot endure his wrath" (Jeremiah 10:10). Notice how Jeremiah connects God's anger and wrath to the eternal kingship of the Lord. Repeatedly we see the truth of these words in the history of humanity. The King was angered when the whole world except a handful of people rebelled against him, and so he brought a worldwide flood and destroyed the entire world of that time (Genesis 6,7). Later when the inhabitants of Sodom and Gomorrah profaned his name by their godless living, he rained fire and brimstone upon those two cities to utterly destroy them (Genesis 19). Or who can forget the ten plagues with which he humbled proud Egypt and her boastful pharaoh (Exodus 7–12)? Even God's own chosen people felt the power of his anger when, after years of patiently seeking their turning from sinful rebellion, he finally crushed the city of Jerusalem by means of the Babylonian invasion (2 Kings 25) and later by means of the Romans. This too is the King to whom we pray.

A compassionate King

Yet Scripture reveals to us more than a king who acts in wrath against the wrongs of our world. He is also, at the same time, a king who shows mercy and compassion time and again. The most outstanding description of this King is found in Exodus 34:6,7, when he revealed himself to Moses as "the LORD, the LORD, the compassionate and gracious God, slow to anger, abounding in love and faithfulness, maintaining love to thousands, and forgiving wickedness, rebellion and sin." These are the characteristics we see when we witness the compassion with which this powerful King treated Adam and Eve. Even after their direct disobedience in the garden, this King gave them the promise of the Savior (Genesis 3:15). This same grace and mercy was evident in the wilderness when the Lord gave Israel manna rather than massacre (Exodus 16). This is the forgiveness that could spare the wicked and rebellious people who inhabited the heathen city of Nineveh (Jonah 3:10). Who but a king who was slow to anger and abounding in love and faithfulness could have put up with the sniveling, complaining, obstinate people of Israel for hundreds of years! This is the King to whom we pray.

Who this King is and what he is like have tremendous implications for our prayers. Since there is no ruler greater than he, he is not controlled by anyone or anything in whatever he chooses to do. Couple this fact with his unlimited power, and we have reason to believe that when we pray to him, there is nothing that he cannot do. This truth, however, must be tempered by the fact that he is a just king. He answers the requests of those who stand in his favor, while he rebukes and even destroys those who incur his anger. "The LORD is far from the wicked but he hears the prayer of the righteous" (Proverbs 15:29). In other words, the sky is the limit for those who please him, but for those who disobey him and reject his rule, there are terrible consequences, which he carries out with absolute authority. Yet even after acknowledging this, there is still reason for those who have disobeyed him to have hope. Without nullifying his justice, he is still the King who shows mercy as he desires and who is unfailing in his love for those over whom he rules.

This, then, is the one to whom we pray. Since he is the Maker and Creator of everything and everyone, he is the King of everything and everyone. To understand and know him is critical if we are going to pray to him. What we know about him will affect our prayers to him. More will be said about this later. First, it is also important to know something about his subjects. The next chapter turns the spotlight on us. We are the ones seeking an audience with the King.

2

The Subjects—Those Seeking an Audience

Status is important

Where we find a king, normally we also expect to find his subjects. So who are the subjects of the King of kings? When we ask that question, the answer we are looking for is not really *who* as in "Who are they?" We already know that everyone everywhere is a subject of this King because he is the only ruler and king over the entire universe. Rather, the question we are really asking when we ask, Who are the subjects of this King? is, What is their status in the kingdom? In ancient kingdoms it made a considerable difference what a person's status was. Some people were considered aristocrats, or the higher ranking people and nobility in a kingdom. Others were considered commoners or even peons—people who were considered very low in the kingdom. Still others were foreigners and had very few rights in the kingdom, if any. Status was important when approaching a king. Some classes of people were not readily allowed into a king's presence. Even those who had the proper status were not allowed to just come into the king's presence anytime they wished. In fact, sometimes it was even considered an offense punishable by death to approach a king with a request if he had not invited you.

Scripture gives us some examples of this relationship between subjects and their kings. In the book of Nehemiah we are told that Nehemiah prayed to the Lord for safety before approaching King Artaxerxes with his request to return to Israel (1:11). Likewise, even Queen Esther was taking a chance when she approached her husband, the king, with her request (Esther 4:11,16). If the king didn't like the request, he could have removed her from her position or even sentenced her to death. Remember that kings were considered to have absolute rule and authority. Their word was law. Not only in foreign lands but also in Israel, there was great respect for the authority of the king. Both Queen Bathsheba and Nathan the prophet bowed before King David with humble respect when they came before him to ask him to carry out his plans to anoint Solomon as his successor (1 Kings 1:15,16,22,23).

These examples remind us of what it means to gain an audience with a king. An audience was a special privilege that was given to someone who held a favorable status with the king. If you were out of the king's favor, you were not granted an audience with him. You could not approach him and make requests of him. Indeed, if you did, you risked your life. So the first question we need to ask if we are going to seek an audience with the King is, What is our status?

The subjects are rebels

The answer may shock us at first: our status is that of rebels who deserve the King's wrath and fury. Who says so? The psalmist who wrote Psalm 14 says so. Paul says so as he echoes the psalmist's words in Romans chapter 3. Ultimately, however, since these men wrote the Word of God, it is God, the King himself, who says this about us. He says, "There is no one who does good. All have turned aside, they have together become corrupt; there is no one who does good, not even one" (Psalm 14:1,3). The wording is all-encompassing. "No one," "all," "together," "not even one" are universal expressions. Paul applies these words to both Jews and Gentiles—which means all humanity. What, therefore, are all the subjects like? They are rebellious. They don't do good. They turn aside from what the King has decreed for them to do. They pervert the morality that he has established for them to live by. In a word, they are disobedient. Need I remind you that *we* are those rebellious subjects?

Such rebelliousness hardly leads to the favorable status that is needed to gain an audience with the King. Rebels do not win kings' favor. Rebels incur their wrath. This is no less true for spiritual rebels, who incur the wrath of the living God. Saint Paul writes in Romans, "The wrath of God is being revealed from heaven against all the godlessness and wickedness of men who suppress the truth by their wickedness" (1:18). Who are the rebels against God whom Paul is speaking about here? Who are these people upon whom the wrath of God is being revealed? Is Paul talking only about people who live in sexual immorality? Does he mean mostly idolaters and murderers? He certainly is talking about those who commit such sins. But the term *rebel* ultimately can be applied to all of us, for by chapter 3 Paul has arrived at the undeniable conclusion that "all have sinned" (verse 23). Therefore, all people are objects of God's wrath. Paul maintains this very thought in Ephesians, where he includes himself and all others in this condemning truth: "we were by nature objects of wrath" (2:3). The King's wrath is fierce. Just as years ago a rebel could simply be dragged out of the king's court to the guillotine or the hangman's noose, so also the wrath of God delivers the sentence of death. The book of Proverbs reminds us, "A king's wrath is like the roar of a lion; he who angers him forfeits his life" (20:2). As if etched in granite at the threshold of the King's court, these words strike terror into the hearts of the rebels who are being brought before the King: "The wages of sin is death" (Romans 6:23).

Rebels have no right to an audience with the King

There is a Latin phrase that we occasionally still run across today. It is the phrase *persona non grata*. It means someone who is out of favor with another person. It is the direct opposite of the favorable status mentioned earlier. In ancient days if someone was labeled *persona non grata*, he was not welcome in the king's court. He had no rights in the kingdom. He certainly was not granted an audience with the king.

The concept of *persona non grata* is somewhat related to the "rogue state" label that we hear about in foreign diplomacy. To be considered a rogue state usually means to not be granted diplomatic or economic privileges. Perhaps trade is limited. By contrast, the most-favored-nation status opens wide the door to free trade. This status declares that there is an agreement between the two nations. They are on good terms with each other.

What is our status before the King? Here we need to understand that by nature our status is *persona non grata*. We are out of favor in the divine court because of our sin. Paul is not heralding good news when he proclaims, "All have sinned and fall short of the glory of God" (Romans 3:23). We are sinners. We have rebelled against the laws of the kingdom. We are therefore outcasts by nature. We are denied an audience. We cannot even hope to enter the King's presence, let alone present a request.

The problem is sin—our sin. Sin is a barrier between us and our King. "Your iniquities have separated you from your God; your sins have hidden his face from you, so that he will not hear" (Isaiah 59:2). We can imagine the agonizing pleas of a young person who has landed himself in jail for the umpteenth time. Disappointed and angered, the father turns away his face, refuses to listen, and walks away, leaving his son in jail. Such is the tragedy Isaiah describes to us here. God will have nothing to do with rebels. As long as sin remains, God, in his holiness, must turn away. So the psalmist also writes, "I cried out to him with my mouth; his praise was on my tongue. If I had cherished sin in my heart, the Lord would not have listened" (66:17,18). The psalmist recognizes that sin is a barrier to an audience with the King. He knows that if he were to revel in his sin, then the King would not listen. Even his praise would be unacceptable if sin remained between them. (We will have more to say about the idea of cherishing sin in the heart in a later chapter.)

Consider also this significant passage from the book of Proverbs:

> Wisdom calls aloud in the street,
>> she raises her voice in the public squares;
> at the head of the noisy streets she cries out,
>> in the gateways of the city she makes her speech:
>
> "How long will you simple ones love your simple ways?
>> How long will mockers delight in mockery
>> and fools hate knowledge?
> If you had responded to my rebuke,
>> I would have poured out my heart to you
>> and made my thoughts known to you.
> But since you rejected me when I called
>> and no one gave heed when I stretched out my hand,
> since you ignored all my advice
>> and would not accept my rebuke,
> I in turn will laugh at your disaster;
>> I will mock when calamity overtakes you—
> when calamity overtakes you like a storm,
>> when disaster sweeps over you like a whirlwind,
>> when distress and trouble overwhelm you.
>
> "Then they will call to me but I will not answer;
>> they will look for me but will not find me.
> Since they hated knowledge
>> and did not choose to fear the LORD,
> since they would not accept my advice
>> and spurned my rebuke,
> they will eat the fruit of their ways
>> and be filled with the fruit of their schemes.
> For the waywardness of the simple will kill them,
>> and the complacency of fools will destroy them;
> but whoever listens to me will live in safety
>> and be at ease, without fear of harm." (1:20-33)

There are several important things to note from this passage. First understand that Wisdom is personified, that is, it is speaking as if it were a person. Wisdom is the Lord's will and ways. In this passage Wisdom is rebuking the "simple ones." This term does not mean people who have below-average IQs. It means those who are morally bankrupt. It means the rebels who deliberately, and not so deliberately at times, violate the rules of the kingdom. Consider carefully how Wisdom longs to speak to these simple ones. She wants to repair the relationship and get back together with the simple ones. But the simple ones refuse. They won't even change when rebuked. They continue in their sins! When calamity and disaster come, however, *then* they want an audience with the King. But what happens? The King won't listen. He won't answer. They won't find him. Why not? Because sin remains between them—unrepented sin.

It appears that the King wants his rebellious subjects to be crystal clear on this issue of status and audience. Over and over we find passages that echo the truth that sin denies us an audience with the King. Another proverb says, "If anyone turns a deaf ear to the law, even his prayers are detestable" (28:9).

The King's refusal to hear the prayers of sinful people is further spelled out by Isaiah. Many of us are familiar with the last words of the following Scripture passage. It is important, however, to also see the context in which these words were spoken.

> "When you spread out your hands in prayer,
>   I will hide my eyes from you;
> even if you offer many prayers,
>   I will not listen.
> Your hands are full of blood;
>   wash and make yourselves clean.
> Take your evil deeds
>   out of my sight!

> Stop doing wrong,
>   learn to do right!
> Seek justice,
>   encourage the oppressed.
> Defend the cause of the fatherless,
>   plead the case of the widow.
> Come now, let us reason together,"
>   says the LORD.
> "Though your sins are like scarlet,
>   they shall be as white as snow;
> though they are red as crimson,
>   they shall be like wool." (Isaiah 1:15-18)

Why does the Lord refuse to listen? Because the people are living in sin. They are not seeking justice. They are oppressing the weak. They are forgetting the orphans. They are ignoring the needs of the widows and allowing these women to be treated unfairly. These actions are evidence of rebellion in the heart. For the actions listed by Isaiah are the things the Lord wants his people to do. These are the things that show harmony between the Lord and his people. The opposite is rebellion. The King will not hear the pleas of rebels.

A similar condemnation against Israel and its leaders was issued by Micah:

> Then I said,
>   "Listen, you leaders of Jacob,
>   you rulers of the house of Israel.
>   Should you not know justice,
>   you who hate good and love evil;
>   who tear the skin from my people
>   and the flesh from their bones;
>   who eat my people's flesh,
>   strip off their skin
>   and break their bones in pieces;

> who chop them up like meat for the pan,
> like flesh for the pot?"
>
> Then they will cry out to the LORD,
> but he will not answer them.
> At that time he will hide his face from them
> because of the evil they have done. (Micah 3:1-4)

The prophet Zechariah spoke the same message about apostate Israel: "'When I called, they did not listen; so when they called, I would not listen,' says the LORD Almighty" (7:13). Here again, notice the Lord's desire to be in harmony with his people. He calls to them. He pleads with them to follow his ways so that he might hear their requests and grant them in full measure. But the people refuse to listen. They ignore the Lord and his will. Then when they are in need and turn to the Lord, he ignores their cries. Their hearts do not belong to the King. They do not cry out as subjects, but as self-serving rebels who use prayer as a means for personal benefit. This is something the King detests.

James reiterates the same point in the New Testament when he chides those who are not receiving the things for which they pray: "When you ask, you do not receive, because you ask with wrong motives, that you may spend what you get on your pleasures" (4:3). It is not just outward sin that is a barrier to our prayers; it is also the motive of our hearts. We are not only rebels because we sin; we are rebels because in our hearts we are not subjects. We are rebels to the core.

As long as sin remains, both in our actions and our attitudes, we remain *persona non grata* by nature and are denied an audience in the courts of the King. And if there is no audience for us in his courts, then there is no answer to our requests. For where there is no audience, no requests can be made. We must first have the right to come into the King's presence before we can hope to have him grant our desires.

What's the use then? How can people who are sinful become unsinful? How can people who are *persona non grata* gain the favor of the King? How can the unworthy become worthy? How will we who are rebels by nature gain an audience with the King, who would crush rebels under his feet? We turn our attention back to the one who is the King.

3

An Audience—The Right to Speak and Be Heard

The King takes action
    The subjects of the King have rebelled. They have no right to be heard. They cannot make themselves acceptable. They are, after all, rebels. The King's wrath burns against them. The only way that they can come into his presence is for the King to desire to have them come. There must be a reconciliation. Their crime, however, is one for which they cannot make amends. *They* cannot reconcile themselves to the King. *He* must reconcile them to himself. He must first put away his burning anger. He must lay aside his sentence of condemnation and treat

them other than as rebels who deserve to die under the laws of the kingdom. For who would approach a tyrant? Who would approach a vengeful king who offers no hope of reconciliation? Isn't it the hope of kindness and mercy that brings subjects before a mighty monarch, even if they have wronged him?

Here is where *the King* is separated from every king who has ever ruled on this earth. What the King of heaven and earth has done for his subjects is something that even the greatest and most benevolent of monarchs on our globe could never do. The King of kings has given an audience to his subjects. To the most stiff-necked of rebels, to us who have taken advantage of his good nature time and again, the King has given the right to be heard. How did this come about?

One had the right to an audience with the King

Our audience with the King came about because there came to this earth one who owned the right to be heard in the court of the King. Daniel speaks about this one as he tells us of an amazing vision he was given by the Lord.

> In my vision at night I looked, and there before me was one like a son of man, coming with the clouds of heaven. He approached the Ancient of Days and was led into his presence. He was given authority, glory and sovereign power; all peoples, nations and men of every language worshiped him. His dominion is an everlasting dominion that will not pass away, and his kingdom is one that will never be destroyed. (Daniel 7:13,14)

Clearly, "the Ancient of Days" is God the Father. He is the King who sits on the throne of heaven. The one "like a son of man" can be none other than Jesus Christ, whom

Scripture says has an everlasting kingdom. Notice that he "approached the Ancient of Days and was led into his presence." Unlike the rebels, who are refused an audience with the King, Jesus is led into the Father's presence. Jesus has the right to an audience with the King.

Jesus is the only subject of the kingdom who inherently has this right. For Jesus is the only subject of the kingdom who by nature pleases the King. Jesus once said, "The one who sent me is with me; he has not left me alone, for I always do what pleases him" (John 8:29). He is perfect in his obedience to all the laws of the kingdom. "During the days of Jesus' life on earth, he offered up prayers and petitions with loud cries and tears to the one who could save him from death, and he was heard because of his reverent submission" (Hebrews 5:7). The glorious Father in heaven, the King of the universe, listens to Jesus and gives him what he asks for. Why? Because Jesus did not rebel against him. Jesus totally and completely submitted to the will of his Father-King. And the Father-King was pleased with him. Both at Jesus' baptism and again at his transfiguration, as his death drew nearer, the Father-King openly declared, "This is my Son, whom I love; with him I am well pleased" (Matthew 3:17; 17:5).

So when Jesus prays to his Father-King, he is always heard. This is according to the King's will. The King never turns a deaf ear to those who please him, to those who are righteous before him. "The eyes of the Lord are on the righteous and his ears are attentive to their prayer" (1 Peter 3:12). Jesus is the only one who can claim to be righteous in himself. Therefore, Jesus never fails to have an audience with the King. Nor was Jesus unaware of this blessed relationship between himself and his Father-King during his days on earth. At Lazarus' tomb Jesus lifted up his voice in prayer to his Father-King and said, "Father, I thank you that you have heard me. I knew that you always hear me, but I said this for the benefit of the people standing here, that they may believe that you sent me" (John 11:41,42).

We need always to keep in mind that *we* have no *inherent* right to an audience with the King. It is not our natural right to pray. The only one who has such an inherent right is Jesus. He has that right by virtue of a sinless life and complete submission to his Father's will.

> As in all other things the fullness dwells in Him, so the true prayer-fullness to[o]; He alone has the power of prayer. And just as the growth of the spiritual life consists in the clearer insight that all the treasures are in Him, and that we too are in Him, to receive each moment what we possess in Him, grace for grace, so with the prayer-life too. Our faith in the intercession of Jesus must not only be that He prays in our stead, when we do not or cannot pray, but that, as the Author of our life and our faith, He draws us on to pray in unison with Himself.[1]

We will have more to say about this last comment and how we pray in unison with Jesus. For now the point must be clearly made that apart from Jesus, we have no inherent right to pray. He is the only one who has this right.

Reconciliation for the rebel

We sinners do not have the inherent right to pray because we are not what Christ Jesus is. We are not acceptable to the King. We are identified as unworthy and denied an audience. We are objects of the King's wrath. So the Bible states with great emphasis: "We were by nature objects of wrath" (Ephesians 2:3). "Whoever believes in the Son has eternal life, but whoever rejects the Son will not see life, for God's wrath remains on him" (John 3:36). The wonderful good news of the first part of this second passage we will discuss in a moment. Carefully examine the second half now. The word "remains" is a key. Where God's wrath remains, it must already have been. There can be no doubt that the King's wrath was once against us, preventing us from any right to be heard.

But the wrath no longer remains on us. This is the message of the first half of that passage. It no longer remains because of Jesus Christ. The prophet, inspired by the Holy Spirit, declares, "He was pierced for our transgressions, he was crushed for our iniquities; the punishment that brought us peace was upon him, and by his wounds we are healed" (Isaiah 53:5). Jesus took the wrath of God on himself. He took our place. The result for us is peace. God's wrath is no longer directed upon us. This is reconciliation.

> All have sinned and fall short of the glory of God, and are justified freely by his grace through the redemption that came by Christ Jesus. God presented him as a sacrifice of atonement [footnote: as the one who would turn aside his wrath, taking away sin], through faith in his blood. He did this to demonstrate his justice, because in his forbearance he had left the sins committed beforehand unpunished—he did it to demonstrate his justice at the present time, so as to be just and the one who justifies those who have faith in Jesus. (Romans 3:23-26)

We love to hear the word *atonement*. It has special significance when we talk about prayer. Those who are not "at one" with God—that is, who are not reconciled, who are still enemies—cannot approach God in prayer. He will grant them no audience. He will not hear. This was our situation. But no more. The King has intervened. He gave Jesus as our "sacrifice of atonement." Note the significance of that phrase as indicated in the footnote. This sacrifice appeased God's anger. It removed his wrath. For Jesus endured God's wrath in the place of all people. The benefits of Jesus' atoning sacrifice are personally received when a person believes in Jesus. So by faith we now stand in Jesus' place—as innocent and right before God. We are at one with God. We are no longer rebels but children who delight him through faith in Jesus. In other words, by faith in Jesus we become what Jesus is to the King. That means that the King will never treat us according to his wrath, as he would treat rebels. "Since we have now been justified by his blood, how much more shall we be saved from God's wrath through him! For if, when we were God's enemies, we were reconciled to him through the death of his Son, how much more, having been reconciled, shall we be saved through his life!" (Romans 5:9,10).

The King grants us an audience

We have now come to a key understanding of the topic of prayer. Prayer is an audience with the King. This audience is unmistakably and inseparably intertwined with justification, that is, with the fact that the King no longer regards us as rebels whom he would just as soon send to the hangman, but rather as dear subjects and sons of his kingdom, whom he has declared innocent of all sin. As one person has defined *justification*, the King sees us "just-as-if" we never rebelled. The King has reconciled *us* to *himself*. "All this is from God, who reconciled us to himself through Christ and gave us the ministry of reconciliation: that God was reconciling the world to himself in Christ, not counting men's sins against them" (2 Corinthians 5:18,19). Peace reigns in the kingdom. Where there is peace, there can now be an audience.

Peace for the rebels is impossible without Jesus Christ. Therefore, only those who believe in Jesus Christ as their Savior from sin have an audience with the King. The King reconciled the world to himself, but this reconciliation came through Christ. Those who reject Jesus lose their audience. By faith in Jesus we become what he is before the King. Jesus is God's most favored Son. By faith in Jesus we receive most-favored-child status with the King. We are no longer *persona non grata*.

The King therefore calls us to repentance. For through repentance the barrier of sin is removed and access to the King's throne is restored.

> When I shut up the heavens so that there is no rain, or command locusts to devour the land or send a plague among my people, if my people, who are called by my name, will humble themselves and pray and seek my face and turn from their wicked ways, then will I hear from heaven and will forgive their sin and will heal their land. Now my eyes will be open and my ears attentive to the prayers offered in this place. I have chosen and consecrated this temple so that my Name may be there forever. My eyes and my heart will always be there. (2 Chronicles 7:13-16)

Here we see how sin affected the audience with the King for ancient Israel. The people had not only sinned against the King, they haughtily refused to admit it. In their typical stiff-necked fashion, they stubbornly refused to acknowledge the cause of the natural disasters that had come upon their land—their sins. Their impenitence left the barrier between themselves and God intact. Therefore, God would not hear. On the other hand, the moment they would come clean before God, the moment they would humble themselves and admit about themselves what God was telling them through the natural disasters and would believe in God's promise of forgiveness, then they would have God's forgiveness. The sincerity of this new attitude would be demonstrated in the ceasing of their sinful activity. This is repentance. Repentance is sorrow over sin together with faith in God's gracious promise of forgiveness for Jesus' sake. Where there is repentance, there is forgiveness of sins. Where sin is forgiven, access to God's throne is restored. This is what the temple represented to the people. It was the King's throne. When they came with repentant hearts, they always received an audience there.

Jesus Christ is our mediator

But just as the people of Israel themselves still could not go into the "throne room" of God, that is, the Most Holy Place of the temple, without the mediation of the high priest, so our access to God's throne also always requires a mediator. That mediator is Jesus Christ. "Since we have been justified through faith, we have peace with God through our Lord Jesus Christ, through whom we have gained access by faith into this grace in which we now stand" (Romans 5:1,2). Jesus is the only mediator for all people. "Through him [Jesus Christ] we both [Jew and non-Jew] have access to the Father by one Spirit" (Ephesians 2:18). It is an unrestricted and unguarded access that Christ has opened for us. "In him and through faith in him we may approach God with freedom and confidence" (3:12).

When the King spoke to his people at Mount Sinai and thundered the Ten Commandments to them out of the dark cloud amidst flashes of lightning, all those present were terrified. They backed away from the mountain and pleaded that Moses should go and speak to the Lord for them and tell them what he said. As long as sin remains, there is fear and uncertainty, which prevents people from approaching the King. This is the same fear that the Lord instilled in his people when he established in their midst the tabernacle and later the temple. Even the high priest was warned about how to approach the Most Holy Place, lest he be destroyed. The high priest was the mediator for the people, yet he was still under the same curse and the same limitations due to his own sins. As long as the temple stood under the old covenant, a curtain remained between the Holy Place and the Most Holy Place. The curtain limited access to the King. It was a constant reminder to the priests and the people that the Lord God was holy and they were not. Open and unhindered dialogue between the King and his people was impossible as long as sin remained.

Then came the Messiah. Jesus Christ was the High Priest of high priests. His access to the throne of God was not hampered by sin. More than that, he gave his life as the payment for the sins of the world. With that sacrifice the barrier between sinful people and the holy God was demolished. Symbolic of this demolition was the tearing of the temple curtain when Jesus died on the cross and the payment of sin was complete (Matthew 27:50,51). The writer to the Hebrews uses the images of the temple and its curtain as he explains to us the wonderful result of Jesus' ultimate sacrifice as our Great High Priest:

> Brothers, since we have confidence to enter the Most Holy Place by the blood of Jesus, by a new and living way opened for us through the curtain, that is, his body, and since we have a great priest over the house of God, let us draw near to God with a sincere heart in full assurance of

faith, having our hearts sprinkled to cleanse us from a guilty conscience and having our bodies washed with pure water. Let us hold unswervingly to the hope we profess, for he who promised is faithful. (Hebrews 10:19-23)

Notice how dependent our access to God's throne is upon the blood of Jesus and his body. This was the payment for our sins. Now that this payment has been made, access is no longer denied. God is no longer angry with us, and guilt need no longer trouble us. Where there is faith in Jesus, there is assurance that the King will hear us and answer our prayers. The way to God's throne is not through some colorful curtain that led to a gold-covered chest. Rather, the way is alive and personal. It is Jesus Christ, and it leads to the very seat of the King himself in heaven.

The same passage that we applied perfectly to Jesus earlier we can now apply also to everyone who believes in Jesus as Savior. "The eyes of the Lord are on the righteous and his ears are attentive to their prayer, but the face of the Lord is against those who do evil" (1 Peter 3:12). We do evil. If there were no Jesus, then the face of the Lord would always be against us. But there is Jesus. Through faith in Jesus, we receive all the blessings that God would bestow on his beloved Son, including total and complete access to his throne in prayer. This is the great message of Jesus' ascension to the right hand of God. By faith we also are seated at God's right hand. Jesus is not only our intercessor, but in him we ourselves also are praying to the Father. By his own word, the Father assures us that he is attentive to our prayers. In Christ we are righteous in God's sight. As Jesus has the right to pray, so we also have that right by faith.

Christ teaches us to pray not only by example, by instruction, by command, by promises, but by showing us HIMSELF, the ever-living Intercessor, as our Life. It is when we believe this, and go and abide in Him for our prayer-life too, that our fears of not being able to pray aright will vanish, and we shall joyfully and triumphantly trust our Lord to teach us to pray, to be Himself the life and the power of our prayer.[2]

The King has become approachable

So the King has become approachable for us. Perhaps you recall a scene from the classic movie *The Wizard of Oz*. This author can remember being terrified as a child at the image of the great and powerful wizard of Oz. Out of the billowing smoke and fire spouts peered the terrible face of the wizard as Dorothy and her friends approached him in the Emerald Palace. Remember how they walked with tiny, fearful steps, knees knocking, down the glass-paneled hallway? The wizard's appearance was not inviting. One so terrifying is not approachable. Who can forget the Tin Man shaking and rattling in fear? Who can forget the moment when the Cowardly Lion finally turns tail, runs frantically down the hall, and jumps through a window? If God appeared to us as the wizard did to Dorothy and her friends, we'd probably respond just like the Tin Man or the Cowardly Lion.

What a difference there is in *The Wizard of Oz* when Dorothy and her friends return from the Wicked Witch of the West's castle to present the broom. At first they appear trembling, as they were at their first visit. Thanks to Toto, however, they soon find that the one who appeared so fearsome was really a kindly old man behind a curtain. Suddenly, he is approachable. Without pushing the illustration too far, it's somewhat similar with God and us. God has not changed. Through Jesus, however, we see God in a new way. Through Jesus, the King whom we knew only as our condemning judge because we rebelled so terribly against his laws is now seen as our benevolent Father. Jesus has revealed to us God's love. For Jesus is evidence of God's incredible love. Jesus is the proof of God's desire to have us as his children.

Jesus has effected this new relationship between the King and us. We are still subjects of his kingdom, but we are much more. To us who were once rebels has been given the title of children of God. Therefore, the King is our heavenly Father. "How great is the love the Father has lavished on us, that we should be called children of God! And that is what we are!" (1 John 3:1). This is the reason Jesus does not teach us to address God as "Oh, almighty and powerful King and Ruler of all." Rather, he tells us to come as children. He teaches us to say "Our Father in heaven."

To say "our Father" to the King is something that only a believer can do. The Holy Spirit, who through faith in Jesus has changed the way we view the King, produces these words in our hearts. "You did not receive a spirit that makes you a slave again to fear, but you received the Spirit of sonship. And by him we cry 'Abba, Father'" (Romans 8:15). "Abba" is the Aramaic word for "father." It is not the same as our children's version of *daddy*. We aren't to think that we have a buddy-buddy relationship with God.[3] As we address our Father in heaven, we never forget that he is the King. What the Spirit teaches us in our hearts through the gospel, however, is that like a dear child, we call the King our Father. The Spirit shows us that, thanks to Jesus and the forgiveness of sins, the relationship we have with the heavenly King is like that between a dear child and a dear father. The father has complete and total love for his child, and the child holds the father dear in love and respect. The child trusts the father implicitly.

Someone may think that the father just described does not sound like his or her human father. This is probably true. Human fathers in our sinful world are not all that God wants fathers to be. Indeed, in many home situations the father is nothing like what God expects a father to be. So the picture may be difficult for some to understand. But that doesn't change the word our Lord Jesus used to teach us about the King. He tells us to call God *our Father*. So we may have to overcome our feelings and experiences toward our earthly fathers to truly understand what Jesus is telling us about our heavenly Father. We must then learn about this Father primarily from what the Bible says about him. We must learn about a true Father from the relationship between Jesus and his Father. There we see perfect love and perfect trust. There we see an endearing relationship filled with mutual respect. This is what we mean when we call the King *our Father*. This is why he is so approachable.

Finally, consider again who it is we are approaching. Though he is our Father, he is still the King. The word *Father* tells us that we are dear to him and that he longs to have us come to him. The word *King* tells us of his power and majesty. The word *Father* tells us that this power and majesty are on our side. They exist for our blessing and our good. Unlike the great and powerful wizard of Oz, who was really just an illusion created by a small man with some elaborate equipment, our God is truly the King of the universe. All things are at his fingertips. This is the one to whom Jesus has opened the door for us. Though approachable, he never ceases to be God Almighty. He is still the King. We have an audience with the King!

What a wonderful thought! We have access to the throne room of the King. Thanks to Jesus, we are standing before the King who is also *our heavenly Father*. What should we say to him? In answer to that question, we will learn in the next chapter that as we come into the throne room, it is necessary that we first listen to what the King says to us. Only if we first listen to what he says to us will we know what we should say to him.

4

The Father-King Speaks First!

God has initiated a conversation with us

Conversations need to be started, that is, someone has to speak first. When two people pass each other in the hallway, they may walk right by each other with neither one saying a word. Then again, perhaps one of them says, "Hi! How are you doing?" but the other person walks by without saying a word. Neither of these situations is a conversation. A conversation takes two people. However, one of them must begin the conversation. Mutual silence never begins a conversation.

Who should begin the conversation when we stand before the King? We might remember a simple rule of etiquette given to young children when they are in the presence of someone important: "Don't speak unless you are spoken to." There is a certain etiquette that does exist in the courtroom of a king. In fact, as we study some of the more noteworthy stories recorded in Scripture regarding the relationship between kings and those around them, we see that there was a set protocol for speaking to a king.

Consider, for example, the account of Queen Esther when she desired to speak to King Xerxes regarding the plot to kill the Jews. Queen Esther did not barge into the king's chambers and begin to air her concerns, even though she was the queen. Rather, we find that not only was she taking a risk coming into the king's presence, but she had to wait for the king's invitation to speak. He began the conversation (Esther 5:2,3). Likewise Queen Bathsheba was not allowed to speak to King David until he had given permission for her to make her request (1 Kings 1:16).

This is the attitude that came to mind for the ancient believer when hearing the word *king* used in reference to someone. Certainly the Lord of heaven and earth uses the title *King* to speak of himself in order to remind us also of an attitude that we must have as we come to him. Even though, through Jesus, the King is most approachable and is in fact our dear Father, yet we dare not come into his presence without due awe and respect. He is still the Maker of heaven and earth. We have been given a tremendous privilege. This does not negate the respect we owe him. The conversation we call *prayer* must be begun by the King. First, we need to listen to what he says. Martin Luther understood this clearly.

> First, we must have a promise or a pledge from God. We must reflect on this promise and remind God of it, and in

that way be emboldened to pray with confidence. If God had not enjoined us to pray and if he had not promised fulfillment, no creature would be able to obtain so much as a kernel of grain despite all his petitions.[4]

Actually, all that we have been learning about the King so far in the previous chapters is what the King has spoken and promised to us. It is from the King himself that we have heard that he loves us, that he has forgiven us and welcomes us into his chambers to speak to him. It is he who invites us and even commands us to respond to his love in prayer, that is, in our part of the conversation that he has begun. It is he who promises to answer our prayers. The King says, "Call upon me in the day of trouble; I will deliver you, and you will honor me" (Psalm 50:15). It is this command and promise of the King in his Word that gives us the courage to come before him in prayer.

The King speaks through his Son

A little later we will discuss what we will say as our side of the conversation. First, let us learn to listen carefully to what the King says. He has much more to say to us. But how and when do we listen to him? Will we hear his voice while we sleep at night? Will he speak to us through prophets?

Here is what the Bible tells us: "In the past God spoke to our forefathers through the prophets at many times and in various ways, but in these last days he has spoken to us by his Son" (Hebrews 1:1,2). Some of the King's conversation with us has been spoken through prophets. They wrote down what the Lord God told them. Countless times they unashamedly declare, "This is what the LORD says." We know the prophets' writings as the books of the Old Testament. A time came, however, when the King wanted to converse with us in a much more intimate way. This he did when Jesus Christ came into our world and spoke with us face-to-face. The "last days" began when Jesus was conceived by the Holy Spirit and born of the virgin Mary. From that day onward, the King has spoken to us by his Son. During his days on earth, Jesus often made statements like this: "These words you hear are not my own; they belong to the Father who sent me" (John 14:24). Jesus is ultimately *the Word* of God, as John calls him in the first chapter of his gospel (verses 1,14). So in order to listen to the King, we need to listen to Jesus Christ, his Son.

Where can we hear Jesus speak to us? Sitting in our 21st-century homes, we wonder how we can hear the voice of Jesus, who spoke two thousand years ago, and thereby first listen to the King. The answer is not difficult, however. The Lord Jesus taught his disciples. He promised them that after he had ascended into heaven and removed his visible presence from earth, he would send them his Holy Spirit to teach them all things and remind them of everything he had said to them (John 14:25,26). And the Holy Spirit did so on Pentecost Sunday. Mightily, Jesus' disciples began to preach and teach—and write. They wrote gospels and letters. In their writings they tell us what Jesus said and did. Here is the answer to our dilemma. How can we hear the King? Through his Son. How can we hear the Son? Through his apostles. How can we hear his apostles? Through the Bible. This means that first we must listen to the Bible. This is the message of God through his Son.

Indeed, until we have heard the King speak to us through his Son, we are not ready to pray. True prayer must flow from the words of Christ.

It is this connection between His word and our prayer that Jesus points to when He says, "If ye abide in me, and my words abide in you, ask whatsoever ye will, and it shall be done unto you." The deep importance of this truth becomes clear if we notice the other expression of which this one has taken the place. More than once Jesus had said, "Abide in me and *I in you*." His abiding in us was the complement and the crown of our abiding in Him. But here, instead of "Ye in me *and I in you*," He says, "Ye in me and *my words in you*." His words abiding are the equivalent of Himself abiding.[5]

Prayer must begin with hearing the Word

In order to pray to the King, then, we first need to hear his Word. If we do not do this, we will not pray properly. In fact, we will not really know and understand the King to whom we wish to speak and make requests. Martin Lehmann makes this observation about Luther and his thoughts:

> In his exposition of Psalm 51 Luther warns explicitly against each and every attempt to seek to know God apart from his Word and promises. Outside of the revelation of his Word we are confronted by "the absolute God," or "the naked God" *(deus nudus)*. Whenever we try to rise to God in our speculations and think of him as he is in himself we risk self-destruction. The revelation of God in Scripture is designed to keep us from pursuing such a dangerous and death-dealing path. For that reason Luther notes that "David is talking with the God of his fathers, with the God who promised." When we search for God in his Word and let him deal with us through the mask of his Word we are on the right track. . . . "We must take hold of this God, not naked but clothed and revealed in His Word; otherwise certain despair will crush us." . . . "This God, clothed in such a kind appearance and, so to speak,

in such a pleasant mask, that is to say, dressed in His promises—this God we can grasp and look at with joy and trust." Such a revelation of God through his Word becomes the basis for true trust in God in the lives of persons, making it possible, yes, necessary for them to speak to God in prayer.[6]

Reading the Bible and prayer

The importance of coupling the reading and hearing of the Word of God to our practice of prayer is something we all need to be reminded of regularly. A survey that this author conducted as part of his research and study for writing this book suggests that we are not remembering this relationship as often as we should.

Allow a brief explanation of the history of this non-scientific survey. This survey was sent to a random sampling of Wisconsin Evangelical Lutheran Synod (WELS) congregations, most of which were in the Midwest. Some were large, and some were small. Some were city congregations; others were rural. There were both established congregations and new missions. From this sampling of congregations, 1,247 surveys were returned and tabulated.

The results of the survey that pertain to the topic at hand are as follows: 98 percent of those who responded said that they prayed at least once a day. Only 33 percent of those who responded, however, said that they read from the Word every day. It is clear that although nearly 100 percent are praying every day, only one-third of these are listening to the King every day. This suggests that we can all do a better job of understanding the need and importance of listening to the King before we begin speaking.

Although the survey question that asked how often people pray each day did not distinguish between mealtime prayers and other prayers, nor did the survey ask how many people read the Bible each week—which may have been considerable—it still seems that such a wide discrepancy between the number of those who pray and the number of those who read the Bible daily is reason for concern. Can we respond correctly if we do not know what the King has said to us first? Is our thanks for our meals proper if we have not first listened to the King tell us where our food comes from and why he gives it to us? Are we requesting the right things? How can we know what the content of our conversation will be unless we have first listened carefully to our King?

Reading the Bible keeps our prayers fresh

Another thing that can happen if we are not first listening to what the King says is that our prayers become stagnant. Like a child who listens to the same song all the time and begins to sing only one song, so our prayers can become a monotonous repetition unless we listen first to the wonderful variation of what the King has to say to us. Consider the lesson learned by George Mueller (1805–1898), a pastor and leader in the Christian Brethren movement in Bristol, England.

> George Mueller of Bristol, England, arose early and gave the first half hour of each day to prayer. After pursuing this course he confessed, however, that his prayers often became shallow and repetitious. It occurred to him that he should first read the Word of God. As he reversed his procedures and spent fifteen or twenty minutes first with the Bible, he found that he never lacked thoughts and words for his prayers.[7]

We've all probably had the experience when every time we talk to a certain person, we hear the same stories or the same conversation. We might wonder why this person doesn't talk about something else for a change. Perhaps part of the reason is that this person hasn't stopped to listen first. There is a real connection between speaking and being a good listener. In fact, the very ability to speak has been linked to hearing.

> Those who have made the deaf and [mute] their study, tell us how much the power of speaking depends on that of hearing, and how the loss of hearing in children is followed by that of speaking too. This is true in a wider sense: as we hear, so we speak. This is true in the highest sense of our intercourse with God. To offer a prayer—to give utterance to certain wishes and to appeal to certain promises—is an easy thing, and can be learned of man by human wisdom. But to pray in the Spirit, to speak words that reach and touch God, that affect and influence the powers of the unseen world—such praying, such speaking, depends entirely upon our hearing God's voice. Just as far as we listen to the voice and language that God speaks, and in the words of God receive His thoughts, His mind, His life, into our heart, we shall learn to speak in the voice and the language that God hears.[8]

Good praying begins with good listening

Being a good listener is the beginning of improving one's prayers. Consider again the insights into prayer that Martin Lehmann learned from Luther:

> Prayer inheres in God's word because the word is spoken to call forth faith and the response of prayer in human hearts. A house of worship, according to Luther, has but one purpose, "that nothing else may ever happen in it except that our dear Lord himself may speak to us through his holy Word and we respond to him through prayer and praise."[9]

Inheres means that prayer must begin in God's Word and remain glued to it. Because prayer, as Luther correctly indicates, is a response of the human heart to what God says in his Word, prayer is really impossible without first listening to what God says.

This relationship can be demonstrated from a familiar passage in Scripture. We remember the command to pray that Jesus gave to his disciples in the Garden of Gethsemane. He told them, "Watch and pray so that you will not fall into temptation" (Mark 14:38). It is clear that one of our defenses against temptation, then, is to turn to God in prayer. But what are we to pray for? Are we to pray for miraculous deliverances? Are we to pray for a magical power to stop us when we are about to fall into temptation? How is temptation overcome? First, it is overcome by the activity of prayer itself. When we are busy praying, then our minds are focused on the Lord, which helps to prevent wayward thoughts.

The greater power of prayer, however, is to pray for the Holy Spirit so that we may have the spiritual understanding and power to recognize and resist temptation. Where does such spiritual understanding come from? How do we learn to recognize temptation? Where does the power to say no come from? It comes from the Word of God. Paul wrote to Titus, "The grace of God that brings salvation has appeared to all men. It teaches us to say 'No' to ungodliness and worldly passions, and to live self-controlled, upright and godly lives in this present age" (2:11,12). From the context of these verses, it is clear that the "grace of God that brings salvation" is something that is known from the teaching of God's Word. In the end, it is God's Word that finally teaches us to say no to temptation. Through the Word, the Holy Spirit strengthens our new self so that we are able to resist temptation. To pray that we will not fall into temptation, then, is to pray, "Lord, convince me of the truth of your Word so that I am not deceived and led astray!" In order to pray this, we first have to know what God's Word says.

When Jesus was tempted in the Garden of Gethsemane, what did he do? He prayed. On what basis did he pray to God? He prayed on the basis of God's Word and promise to him. When Jesus finally said, "Not my will, but yours be done" (Luke 22:42), he showed that he had found the answer and defense against temptation in God's Word. He had become convinced of the truth and faithfulness of God and the reliability of his Word. He trusted in that Word, rather than the deceptions of Satan. Do you see how prayer and listening go together? When Jesus prayed that God might remove the cup of suffering from him, he at the same time listened to the Word of God that said he must drink it. His prayer, therefore, correctly responded by saying, "Not my will, but yours be done."

The Sixth Petition of the Lord's Prayer is "Lead us not into temptation." When Luther explains this petition in his Small Catechism, he says that we are praying "that God would guard and keep us, so that the devil, the world, and our flesh may not deceive us or lead us into false belief, despair, and other great and shameful sins." How does God guard and keep us from false belief, despair, and other great and shameful sins? Through his Word! The Word of God tells us what is true belief. The Word of God fills us with hope in the midst of severe temptations. The Word of God shows us the path to walk so that we do not walk in the way of sinners. In order to pray this petition, we first need to know what God's Word tells us. We won't even know what we are praying until we first know what

God tells us in his Word about how to overcome temptations. Once we know what his Word says, then we are ready to respond with our prayers and requests, asking him to help us in the very way he has told us he will.

Some misconceptions about prayer

"Last night while I was praying, God told me to sell our home and move." Have you ever heard someone say something like this? Such a statement betrays a misconception about prayer. Some people expect God to speak to them directly while they are praying.

As we have seen, however, God speaks to us through his Word in the Bible. If we want to be guided by God, we need to know the Scriptures. We have no promise from God that he will talk to us directly in prayer or in any way apart from his Word in the Bible. Prayer, on the other hand, is our opportunity to talk to him.

Once we have learned to listen to the King, then we are ready to begin our side of the conversation. This is what we commonly refer to as prayer. It is our response to the Word of the King.

5

We Speak to the King

Herbert Lockyer calls prayer "heaven's telephone, free to all, always disengaged, never out of order."[10] So it is. The King has dialed our number. He has spoken first in words of hope and invitation. Now he pauses to hear what we have to say. He stays on the line. He doesn't hang up. He waits to hear from us.

Prayer is a response to the King

At last we have come to prayer itself. It is now time for the subjects to speak, to respond to what the King says. There are several responses that might take place. There might simply be informal responses to what the King has just said. Perhaps a tear at his words of forgiveness. Perhaps a smile at the sound of his love. Maybe a sigh at his comforting assurances. Or maybe even a boisterous "Alleluia!" at the good news of victory and freedom. These informal responses in themselves are prayer. They are a response to the communication of the King to his subjects. As James Montgomery wrote in his hymn, "Prayer is the burden of a sigh, the falling of a tear, the upward glancing of an eye, when none but God is near."[11]

Most commonly, however, prayer is more than nonverbal communication. Prayer takes place when the subjects begin to speak. Or, because the listener is divine, prayer need not even be expressed with words but simply takes the form of thoughts that are directed to the One who knows even our inmost musings. It is to such prayer that our attention now turns.

Prayer is worship

First, it is important for us to remember that prayer is worship. Paul wrote to the Romans, "I urge you, brothers, in view of God's mercy, to offer your bodies as living sacrifices, holy and pleasing to God—this is your spiritual act of worship" (12:1). Here Paul wants us to understand that as we respond to God's mercy, we are worshiping him. Prayer, as we have already noted, is a response to the King's message to us. It is return conversation that has been prompted by the merciful message of the gospel. Therefore, prayer is worship, whether individual prayer or group prayer. It is the service of our hearts and lips as opposed to the service of our hands and feet. Paul wants us to offer our whole bodies to God in service. This includes our minds and our voices. So when we pray, we worship. We serve God.

Prayer-worship takes different forms

Praise

The worship we render God in prayer can take many different forms, as is evident in the prayers recorded in the Bible. There are different reasons and ways to communicate with the King. Yet each of these ways of communication can in a general way be called prayer. For example, our prayer might take the form of praise, as in the following passages from Psalms:

> Sing to the LORD a new song,
>   for he has done marvelous things;
> his right hand and his holy arm
>   have worked salvation for him.
> Shout for joy to the LORD, all the earth,
>   burst into jubilant song with music. (98:1,4)

> Sing to the LORD, praise his name;
>   proclaim his salvation day after day. (96:2)

> Praise the LORD, O my soul;
>   all my inmost being, praise his holy name.
> Praise the LORD, O my soul,
>   and forget not all his benefits. (103:1,2)

Thanks

Prayer may also simply be an expression of our thanks to God for blessings he has given us. The following passages are examples of thanksgiving prayers:

> Give thanks to the LORD, for he is good.
>   His love endures forever. (Psalm 136:1)

> I thank and praise you, O God of my fathers:
>   You have given me wisdom and power,
> you have made known to me what we asked of you,
>   you have made known to us the dream of the king.
>   (Daniel 2:23)

He directed the people to sit down on the grass. Taking the five loaves and the two fish and looking up to heaven, he gave thanks and broke the loaves. Then he gave them to the disciples, and the disciples gave them to the people. (Matthew 14:19)

We always thank God, the Father of our Lord Jesus Christ, when we pray for you. (Colossians 1:3)

Confession of sin

Another form of prayer is when our communication with God recognizes the truth of what he tells us about our sinful natures. When that happens, our hearts begin to pour out words that say "I'm sorry" and ask for forgiveness. This is what we call *confession*. Here are a few examples:

> When I kept silent,
>   my bones wasted away
>   through my groaning all day long.
> For day and night
>   your hand was heavy upon me;
> my strength was sapped
>   as in the heat of summer.
> Then I acknowledged my sin to you
>   and did not cover up my iniquity.
> I said, "I will confess
>   my transgressions to the LORD"—
> and you forgave
>   the guilt of my sin.
> Therefore let everyone who is godly pray to you
>   while you may be found. (Psalm 32:3-6)

> Have mercy on me, O God,
>   according to your unfailing love;
> according to your great compassion
>   blot out my transgressions.

> Wash away all my iniquity
> and cleanse me from my sin.
> For I know my transgressions,
> and my sin is always before me.
> Against you, you only, have I sinned
> and done what is evil in your sight. . . .
> Cleanse me with hyssop, and I will be clean;
> wash me, and I will be whiter than snow.
> (Psalm 51:1-4,7)

> O my God, I am too ashamed and disgraced to lift up my face to you, my God, because our sins are higher than our heads and our guilt has reached to the heavens. From the days of our forefathers until now, our guilt has been great. (Ezra 9:6,7)

> O LORD, God of heaven, the great and awesome God, who keeps his covenant of love with those who love him and obey his commands, let your ear be attentive and your eyes open to hear the prayer your servant is praying before you day and night for your servants, the people of Israel. I confess the sins we Israelites, including myself and my father's house, have committed against you. We have acted very wickedly toward you. We have not obeyed the commands, decrees and laws you gave your servant Moses. (Nehemiah 1:5-7)

Requests

Prayers can also simply be requests for gifts and blessings that we ask of our King. Consider these examples:

> O LORD Almighty, if you will only look upon your servant's misery and remember me, and not forget your servant but give her a son, then I will give him to the LORD for all the days of his life, and no razor will ever be used on his head. (1 Samuel 1:11)

> If you will save Israel by my hand as you have promised—look, I will place a wool fleece on the threshing floor. If there is dew only on the fleece and all the ground is dry, then I will know that you will save Israel by my hand, as you said. (Judges 6:36,37)

Intercessions

Finally, prayers can be for others. We call this type of prayer *intercession* since we are interceding with the King on behalf of others. Scripture also records these types of prayers:

> Oh, what a great sin these people have committed! They have made themselves gods of gold. But now, please forgive their sin—but if not, then blot me out of the book you have written. (Exodus 32:31,32)

> Pray to the LORD your God for your servants so that we will not die, for we have added to all our other sins the evil of asking for a king. (1 Samuel 12:19)

> Far be it from me that I should sin against the LORD by failing to pray for you. (verse 23)

> Father, forgive them, for they do not know what they are doing. (Luke 23:34)

Prayer is a special kind of communication

As can be seen from the examples above, prayer covers many different kinds of conversation that the believer might carry on with God. Yet, though we defined prayer as communication with God, it is not the same kind of conversation that we casually carry on with the clerk across the checkout counter or with our next-door neighbor across the fence. Prayer, ultimately, is conversation that is carried on with our *Father-King*. Such conversation has a unique flavor to it that is not true of any other kind of conversation in which we engage. This is why we don't commonly call conversation with other people "prayer." We usually reserve the word *prayer* to speak of the conversation that we carry on with our God, the King.

The most common words used for *prayer* in both the Old and New Testaments, that is, in both the Hebrew and Greek languages, strongly suggest a very special kind of communication that we carry on with the King. It is not within the scope of this book to list all the Hebrew or Greek words for *prayer* and all the passages in which they are used. Let it suffice to say that after a study of the various words used for *prayer* and the contexts in which they occur, one common theme began to present itself to this author. In the contexts of the two most common words for *prayer* in the Hebrew and the Greek, there always seems to be some connection with the idea of seeking divine favor by those who are not worthy of that favor. In other words, God's mercy and undeserved love—what we call grace—are always at the heart of prayer.

Consider the wording of this passage: "The LORD has heard my cry for mercy; the LORD accepts my prayer" (Psalm 6:9). Hebrew poetry uses a technique called parallelism. This means that in most verses of Hebrew poetry, the first half and the second half have a special connection or relationship with each other. Sometimes they say the same thing. Sometimes the second half adds a thought to the first or contrasts it. The passage quoted above is of the type where the second half repeats what the first half said, only in slightly different words. In such passages we often gain insight into the relationships of important concepts in the Bible. Notice in the passage above that the words "heard" and "accepts" are used basically as synonyms. To say that the Lord hears my prayers is also to say that he accepts them. In the same way, notice the parallel structure between the phrases "my cry for mercy" and "my prayer." The word for *prayer* here is the most common Hebrew word for *prayer*. From the parallel structure we see that it is used synonymously with "cry for mercy." This suggests a close relationship between prayer and seeking God's mercy. It reminds us that we are unworthy subjects coming to the glorious King. At the same time it reminds us that, thanks to Jesus, we have the assurance that God is merciful to us and does hear our prayers.

Another example of this relationship between prayer and God's grace and mercy is found in James' letter. Near the close of his letter, James writes, "Elijah was a man just like us. He prayed earnestly that it would not rain, and it did not rain on the land for three and a half years. Again he prayed, and the heavens gave rain, and the earth produced its crops" (5:17,18). James makes a point of noting that Elijah was a man just like us. He was mortal. He had no special powers within himself. Clearly, the object of his prayer was the Lord, the King. His prayer, however, was more than a casual conversation. James says Elijah prayed earnestly. This indicates that Elijah was seeking something from the Lord and was seeking it with great passion. On the surface, he was asking the Lord to prevent it from raining. This was such a bold and unusual request, however, that Elijah prayed earnestly. He was really seeking divine favor. Only if the Lord looked upon this mortal with favor would he grant such a bold request. James notes that twice Elijah's requests were granted. The Greek word here is the most common word for *prayer*. In the context, it is connected to the thought of seeking divine favor.

Prayer always seeks divine favor

As we define *prayer*, then, we will want to keep in mind that part of the definition of *prayer* is that it is a seeking of divine favor. Moses reminded the people of Israel as they were at the border of the Promised Land, "I prayed to the LORD and said, 'O Sovereign LORD, do not destroy your people, your own inheritance that you redeemed by your great power and brought out of Egypt with a mighty hand'" (Deuteronomy 9:26). This prayer arose because the people had rebelled against God and worshiped the golden calf. God's anger had been aroused against them. Why should God now put away his anger? Why should God allow them to live rather than destroy them? Moses wasn't simply making a request of God. He was imploring God's mercy. He was asking for God to show favor and love that was undeserved rather than the punishment that was deserved.

In the days of Eli the priest, there was a woman named Hannah. We are told in Scripture, "In bitterness of soul Hannah wept much and prayed to the LORD" (1 Samuel 1:10). Hannah desperately wanted a son, but she had none. In those days it was a disgrace for a woman not to have children. Many believed it was a divine rebuke or a sign of divine displeasure. Hannah was not just asking for a son as she prayed. She was imploring God to look upon her with favor.

As we look at prayer after prayer in the Old Testament, we find again and again that in one way or another the person who is praying is seeking divine favor. Abraham sought God's mercy on Abimelech for the way he treated Sarah (Genesis 20:17,18). Solomon prayed for mercy upon the people at the dedication of the magnificent new temple of the Lord. The whole purpose of the temple was that the people might now come to this house of God to seek divine favor. Solomon pleaded in his prayer that the Lord would remember his promises and forgive his people. He is asking for mercy (1 Kings 8). Elisha asked for divine favor on the Shunammite woman whose son died (2 Kings 4:33). Hezekiah asked for divine favor and mercy when he prayed to the Lord that he might be healed from his illness and live longer (2 Kings 20:2,3). Manasseh, one of the most wicked kings of Judah, pleaded for mercy for all the wickedness he had done (2 Chronicles 33:12,13). Surely, he had no right to expect anything good from the Lord. Yet he prayed. He sought divine favor. Nehemiah pleaded that the Lord would forgive the exiles and allow the walls of Jerusalem to be rebuilt (Nehemiah 1:4-11). Jonah prayed from the belly of the fish (Jonah 2:2-9). He was in distress. His only hope was that the Lord, against whom he had sinned and from whom he was running, would be merciful. If he was to experience deliverance, it would be because the Lord was showing him favor he didn't deserve. The psalmists likewise again and again cry out for help from the Lord. Their prayers are essentially cries for mercy. Help will be provided only if the Lord looks upon them favorably. To ask for help is to ask the Lord to show them mercy.

So far, we have looked primarily at the Hebrew word for *prayer*. Its Greek counterpart in the New Testament is used in a similar fashion. For example, we read in Acts chapter 12, "Peter was kept in prison, but the church was earnestly praying to God for him" (verse 5). Peter was in prison. He was in dire need of help. We are told that the fledgling Christian church was praying for him. These believers were not, however, merely conversing with God about Peter. They were asking the Lord to show him favor—to protect him or perhaps even see to his release if that was the Lord's will.

Another example is found in Paul's exhortation to the Christians in Philippi. "Do not be anxious about anything, but in everything, by prayer and petition, with thanksgiving, present your requests to God" (Philippians 4:6). Clearly, his fellow believers were anxious about many things. Prayer is speaking to God, which anxious people need to do—namely, asking for God's favor in time of need.

In his letter to the congregation in Colosse, Paul wrote, "Epaphras, who is one of you and a servant of Christ Jesus, sends greetings. He is always wrestling in prayer for you, that you may stand firm in all the will of God, mature and fully assured" (Colossians 4:12). Here we see that Epaphras was "wrestling" for something. This wrestling was not a physical wrestling but a wrestling done in prayer. The specific thing for which Epaphras was wrestling is spelled out. He was begging God by means of prayer to help his brothers and sisters in the faith "stand firm in all the will of God." His prayer then was for God's favor on the congregation in Colosse. He wanted the Lord to bless them.

Again, it can be seen that in both the New Testament and the Old Testament, the most common words for *prayer* carry the essence of asking for the Lord's favor. In fact, this thought can be inserted into nearly every context in which the common word for *prayer* is used without disrupting the sense of the sentence. This fact alone reminds us of the need for Jesus Christ when we pray. For without Jesus it is futile to seek divine favor. Only because of and through Jesus Christ and his merits does the Lord ever look favorably upon sinners. So every prayer that we pray must begin with the realization of our unworthiness to pray. At the same time, our hearts and souls must grasp the wonderful message of the gospel. For Jesus' sake God shows us undeserved love (grace) and therefore gladly hears and answers our prayers. He *does* show us favor.

This is what Luther conveys to us in his explanation to the Fifth Petition of the Lord's Prayer. We might think it strange that Luther speaks of prayer in the petition that says "Forgive us our sins, as we forgive those who sin against us." Yet it is here, with forgiveness, that our prayers begin and end. How simply Luther recognizes this when he explains in the Small Catechism, "We pray in this petition that our Father in heaven would not look upon our sins or because of them deny our prayers; for we are worthy of none of the things for which we ask, neither have we deserved them, but we ask that he would give them all to us by grace; for we daily sin much and surely deserve nothing but punishment." Luther knows what the Bible says about sin and prayer. Where there is unforgiven sin, there can be no prayer—that is, no requests that reach the Father's ears and are answered. Sin is a barrier between us and our King. We beg our Father in heaven not to look upon our sin. Notice that Luther admits that we still sin—daily and much. We still deserve only God's wrath and punishment. We have not changed. We are praying, however, that the King would not see us as we are but would see us through our Savior, Jesus Christ. This is the prayer of faith. It believes and trusts that our Father-King does look upon us favorably with grace (undeserved love) and therefore will grant our petitions.

Only believers in Jesus can pray

This is an important thing to remember: those who do not believe in Jesus Christ cannot truly pray. They cannot seek the favor of the King because their sins still separate them from the King. This is the consistent message of the Bible, as passage after passage speaks of prayer. Prayer is always connected with faith in Jesus.

In Psalm 32, for example, we read, "Let everyone who is godly pray to you while you may be found" (verse 6). The psalmist doesn't say, "Let everyone pray." He qualifies "everyone" with the word "godly." This word indicates those who are God's kind of people. These are not perfect people. They are penitent people who do not trust in their own merit or worthiness but look to Jesus as their Savior and the reason for God's good favor. These people, the godly, can and do pray to God and find him in his words and promises.

Another psalm passage echoes this truth. In Psalm 145 we read, "The LORD is near to all who call on him, to all who call on him in truth" (verse 18). Once more there is a qualifier attached to those who call on the Lord. They must call on the Lord in truth. The Bible teaches us that God's Word is truth (John 17:17). Jesus also called himself the Truth (John 14:6). So those who call on the Lord in truth are those who listen to God's Word and believe the truth about Jesus that it reveals. In short, they believe the gospel promises of God about Jesus. For them, God is near.

Near the end of his first letter to the Christians in Thessalonica, Paul gives a series of encouragements to this beleaguered congregation. "Be joyful always; pray continually; give thanks in all circumstances, for this is God's will for you in Christ Jesus" (1 Thessalonians 5:16-18). The three commands that Paul gives them are all related to the last clause, which tells these Christians that this is what God wants them to do. However, Paul adds the words "in Christ Jesus." This is a reminder that our joy, our prayers, and our giving thanks are all possible only because of and through Jesus Christ. Unless we first know and believe in Jesus Christ, we cannot pray as God wants us to. Faith in Jesus comes first. Prayer is the language of faith.

God pictured this truth to his Old Testament believers through the layout of the tabernacle and, later, of the temple in Jerusalem. The people were separated from the Most Holy Place. Yet it was in the Most Holy Place that God was present among them. There they could lift up their prayers to him. The only way to God, however, was through the sacrifices and the blood that the priests sprinkled on the altar and that the high priest sprinkled once a year on the ark of the covenant. These things were symbols and pictures to teach God's people of old about the coming Messiah.

The writer to the Hebrews later uses these pictures to help us understand the wonderful relationship we now have with God—particularly the access we have to God in prayer through Jesus.

> Brothers, since we have confidence to enter the Most Holy Place by the blood of Jesus, by a new and living way opened for us through the curtain, that is, his body, and since we have a great priest over the house of God, let us draw near to God with a sincere heart in full assurance of faith, having our hearts sprinkled to cleanse us from a guilty conscience and having our bodies washed with pure water. (10:19-22)

The writer says that we have the "full assurance of faith" to approach God in prayer. We are not afraid of being turned away. We are not afraid of being sentenced to death. We are not afraid of the King's wrath. Why not? Because of Jesus. Because Jesus shed his blood and gave his body for us on the cross. When this passage says that our hearts are sprinkled and our bodies are washed, this means that God has applied to us the forgiveness and righteousness that Jesus earned. This is what we call *justification*. To have confidence in this is to believe it. That's faith. We pray because we believe this is true. We believe that through Jesus, God's house of prayer is open to us.

Can unbelievers pray? Certainly, they can say words that sound like prayers. They can even call upon God with the right terminology. But because they do not believe in Jesus as their Savior from sin, their prayers will not be heard or accepted. For without Jesus as the go-between, the mediator, unbelievers themselves and whatever they do, including their prayers, are not acceptable or pleasing to God. "Without faith it is impossible to please God" (Hebrews 11:6). This is the clear teaching of God's Word. Unbelievers cannot pray in the biblical sense of the word. A comment by the great theologian Augustine is appropriate here:

> Because he [Paul] said, 'How are they to call upon him in whom they have not believed?' you have not first been taught the Lord's Prayer, and then the Creed. You have been taught the Creed first, so that you may know what to believe, and afterwards the Prayer, so that you may know upon whom to call. The Creed contains what you are to believe; the Prayer, what you are to ask for. It is the believer's prayer that is heard.[12]

Without faith in Jesus Christ, it is impossible to pray. On the other hand, when a person comes to believe in Jesus Christ, then it impossible *not* to pray. The moment that the Holy Spirit produces faith in the heart through the gospel, prayers begin to spring from the Christian's heart and lips. Luther once said, "A Christian without prayer is just as impossible as a living person without a pulse. The pulse is never motionless; it moves and beats constantly, whether one is asleep or something else keeps one from being aware of it."[13] This vital link between faith and prayer simply follows the Lutheran teaching on the relationship between justification, or our becoming a Christian, and sanctification, or our living as a Christian. Sanctification can never precede justification. We cannot live like Christians and do what Christians do until we are Christians. Once a person becomes a Christian by God's grace and the power of the Holy Spirit, however, at that very same moment that person begins to act like a Christian. That includes the heartfelt desire to pray.

So the Christian, the believer, begins to pray. For whom will we pray? What will we pray about? We will take up these questions in the next chapter as we consider the requests that we, God's children and subjects, bring to our Father-King.

6

We Bring Our Requests to the King

We pray for ourselves

For whom will we pray? To begin with, for ourselves. "If you then, though you are evil, know how to give good gifts to your children, how much more will your Father in heaven give the Holy Spirit to those who ask him!" (Luke 11:13). Jesus spoke these words to his disciples at a time when they had asked him to teach them how to pray. First he gave them a model prayer, now known as the Lord's Prayer, which we will discuss later in this book. Following that, he used an illustration to teach them to be persistent when they prayed to the Father in heaven and to not give up after the first time. In conclusion to this illustration,

Jesus spoke the words that have been quoted on the previous page. The point is that just as children ask their fathers for things for themselves, and the fathers know enough to give good gifts to their children, so also when we ask for things for ourselves from our heavenly Father, he will surely give us good gifts. He is far better than our earthly fathers, who are not perfect but are evil by nature. Self-understood in this assurance is the fact that we are permitted and encouraged to pray for our own needs. Jesus indicates that asking for the Holy Spirit is to be foremost. This is the best and most important gift that our heavenly Father desires to give to his children.

The gospel of Matthew records for us an account where Jesus was telling his disciples about the impending destruction of Jerusalem and the final destruction of the whole world. Knowing the terrible nature of these destructions, Jesus implores them, "Pray that your flight will not take place in winter or on the Sabbath" (24:20). Clearly, Jesus was telling the disciples to pray for their own benefit. It is for self-preservation and protection that they were to seek God's favor.

Again, in Luke's gospel we have an example of Jesus commanding his disciples to pray for themselves. Jesus was in the Garden of Gethsemane praying for himself. When he found his disciples sleeping, he said to them, "Get up and pray so that you will not fall into temptation" (22:46). Jesus was not telling them here to pray for someone else, but for themselves. How important it is that we pray for ourselves against temptation! Without the Lord's help, we will surely fall into temptation.

> No one escapes the trials of life. By recourse to prayer we can entreat God for help in the midst of them. In this

connection Luther relates from Jerome's *Lives of the Hermits* how a young hermit who desired to get rid of his unwholesome thoughts was told by his older companion, "Dear brother, you cannot prevent the birds from flying over your head, but you can certainly keep them from building a nest in your hair." Our prayers for divine assistance can help us in overcoming the temptations which assail us.[14]

Another prayer we might offer for ourselves would be a prayer for forgiveness. Simon the Sorcerer was commanded by Peter to pray such a prayer after he had sinned by trying to buy the ability to give the Holy Spirit through the laying on of hands. "Repent of this wickedness and pray to the Lord. Perhaps he will forgive you for having such a thought in your heart" (Acts 8:22).

Prayer for ourselves is appropriate in any situation where we need the Lord's help. James gives a general command when he says, "Is any one of you in trouble? He should pray" (5:13). Paul likewise is generalizing when he exhorts, "Do not be anxious about anything, but in everything, by prayer and petition, with thanksgiving, present your requests to God" (Philippians 4:6). The two words "anything" and "everything" open the door wide to any number of things that Christians might pray about to their Father-King.

We pray for others

Our prayers, however, are not to be limited to ourselves and our own needs. Just as forcefully as Scripture teaches us to pray for ourselves, it also teaches us unmistakably to lift our voices to the King on behalf of others. "I urge, then, first of all, that requests, prayers, intercession and thanksgiving be made for everyone—for kings and all those in authority, that we may live peaceful and quiet lives in all godliness and holiness" (1 Timothy 2:1,2). Paul piles an interesting group of words together here as he exhorts us to pray for others. The words suggest that we are to ask for gifts, for divine favor, and for forgiveness, and that we are even to give thanks for others. The particular focal point of our prayers in this verse is the government—presidents, governors, police, judges, legislators, mayors, and the like. We are commanded to pray for them so that our lives may remain peaceful and quiet for the proclamation of the gospel. This seems to suggest that we pray that these individuals in authority may be given such things as common sense and the ability to rule fairly and justly, or perhaps even that they may come to faith if they are not already Christians.

A prayer for coming to faith was just what Paul had in mind when he stood before King Agrippa II. In the book of Acts we are told that after Paul had witnessed to Agrippa about Christ, Agrippa skirted Paul's question and said that Paul wasn't going to convert him so quickly. Paul responded, "Short time or long—I pray God that not only you but all who are listening to me today may become what I am, except for these chains" (26:29).

We are not only to pray for unbelievers, though. We are also enjoined by God's Word to pray for our fellow believers, especially for those who are proclaiming the gospel. Paul wrote to his Christian brothers and sisters at Rome, "I urge you, brothers, by our Lord Jesus Christ and by the love of the Spirit, to join me in my struggle by praying to God for me. Pray that I may be rescued from the unbelievers in Judea and that my service in Jerusalem may be acceptable to the saints there" (Romans 15:30,31).

Our prayers for others need not be limited to prayers for the spread of the gospel. James urges prayers for others in times of illness: "Is any one of you sick? He should call the elders of the church to pray over him and anoint him with oil in the name of the Lord" (5:14). This passage is important because it teaches us to seek the prayers of others on our behalf. This is one of the great blessings of the holy Christian church. Since we are a communion of saints—that is, we are bound together by one faith in Jesus Christ and one Spirit, who effects that faith—Christians are deeply involved in one another's lives. This includes active and fervent prayers for one another. "Confess your sins to each other and pray for each other so that you may be healed. The prayer of a righteous man is powerful and effective" (James 5:16). Only fellow Christians in the holy Christian church can offer such powerful and effective prayers. For "a righteous man," as Scripture teaches, is only someone who has the righteousness of God through faith in Jesus Christ. So another way of saying this would be, "The prayer of someone who has confessed his sins and trusts in Jesus Christ as his Savior is powerful and effective." Believers therefore pray for one another as James has commanded.

The foremost example of prayer for others is given us by the perfect and righteous Savior himself. The 17th chapter of John's gospel contains an extended prayer of Jesus in which he prays for himself, his disciples, and believers of all time. It is worth reading as a model to us of prayer for others. Another example would be Jesus' prayer for Peter (Luke 22:32). Jesus knew that Peter was going to be sorely tempted by Satan. So he prayed that Peter would overcome and his faith would be sustained.

As in all things, we are to pattern our Christian lives after the model that Christ has given us. This is no less true in prayer. In his book *Luther and Prayer*, Martin Lehman summarizes Luther's thoughts on this point as follows:

> Because Jesus Christ intercedes for us before God, we, too, should intercede for others in prayer in his name and spirit. A Christian dare not restrict his prayers to himself or to the narrow circle of his family or friends. His prayers are so all-encompassing in their scope, even as Christ was concerned about and prayed for all sorts and conditions of people.[15]

In a certain sense, a prayer for other Christians is really a prayer for oneself. This is because Jesus calls all Christians his body. Every Christian is part of that body and is therefore affected by whatever happens to that body. When we pray for other believers, we are praying for the body of Christ, of which we are a part and beneficiary. In this regard, Luther states,

> So then, true love will prompt us to pray above all else for Christendom, and this accomplishes more than praying just for ourselves. For, as Chrysostom says, all of Christendom prays for him who prays for it. Indeed, in such a prayer he prays together with Christendom for himself. . . . I ask you to note and ponder that it is not without reason that Christ taught us to pray "our Father" and not "my Father," "give us this day our daily bread" and not "my daily bread," that he speaks of "our trespasses," "us," and "our." He wants to hear the throngs and not me or you alone, or a single isolated Pharisee. Therefore sing with the congregation and you will sing well. Even if your singing is not melodious, it will be swallowed up by the crowd. But if you sing alone you will have your critics.[16]

The saying "No man is an island" is truest in the Christian church. Believers will pray for one another.

Perhaps what shocks us a bit more than hearing the Lord Jesus tell us to pray for fellow believers is his will that we pray also for our enemies and those who persecute us. "I tell you: Love your enemies and pray for those who persecute you" (Matthew 5:44). "Bless those who curse you, pray for those who mistreat you" (Luke 6:28). Praying for others is clearly extended by Jesus beyond the walls of our church, our synod, and even Christianity. "Others" includes those we would rather not pray for. It includes those who do us harm and cause us pain and suffering. Nor are the prayers that we utter for these people to be tit-for-tat exercises. Jesus is certainly not telling us to pray for their demise when he says, "Love your enemies and pray for those . . ." Our prayers for our enemies are to be the fruit of forgiven hearts that have been touched by God's forgiving love and mercy. We, in turn, show mercy and pray for forgiveness upon those who have wronged us in any way. Our Savior shows us how. When the soldiers crucified him, he pleaded for forgiveness for those who thought nothing of pounding nails through the hands of the Son of God (Luke 23:34). This type of prayer does not come easily to us. This type of prayer is forged in the furnace of repentance (sorrow over sins) and absolution (forgiveness). Too often we would withhold what the Father-King has so freely given to us. Only by staring into the mirror of God's law and then basking in the light of the cross and the empty tomb will we be empowered to forgive and pray for our enemies.

Finally, also singled out for special attention are prayers for little children. Our Savior himself prayed for the little children. The Holy Spirit saw fit to record the Savior's activity so that we might learn from his example. In Matthew's gospel we are told, "Then little children were brought to Jesus for him to place his hands on them and pray for them. But the disciples rebuked those who brought them" (19:13). You may recall that Jesus rebuked the disciples for stopping those who brought their children. He took the children in his arms and blessed them. People were bringing them to Jesus to have him pray for them because this is what Jesus did. He prayed for the little children. So also we are to pray for little children—that they would be protected, that their faith would grow, that they would be saved.

There is one group for whom we have no encouragement to pray, however. That group is the dead. We know that each person faces judgment at the point of death (Hebrews 9:27), and one's eternal destiny in heaven or hell cannot be changed after death. Therefore, it is useless to offer prayers to help the souls of people who have died. Certainly, we may offer prayers of thanksgiving to God for blessings received during the life of one who has died. But there is no command or promise of God in the Bible associated with prayers to help the dead, nor is there any example of such prayer. The Roman Catholic Church supports its custom of prayers for the dead with a passage from the Apocrypha (2 Maccabees 12:43-45), not from the Bible.

The Holy Spirit helps us pray

As we near the end of this chapter in which we see for whom and for what we are to pray to our King, we may feel a bit overwhelmed. We may feel that in our human weakness, we often fail to exercise this wonderful privilege or that when we do, we do so only feebly. As in all our Christian living, we struggle and stumble rather than coast. Luther addresses these feelings of inadequacy with a startling assertion that can only be made by someone who knows the truth and promises of God most clearly. Martin Lehmann offers a summary of Luther's insight into our human weakness and the Spirit's power working through our prayers. Humbled by their weaknesses and inadequacies, Christians are conscious of their helplessness.

> "Then they [Christ's disciples] will exercise their faith all the more by prayer and petition, and will experience His power in weakness and in suffering the more surely, because they will be impelled to call upon Him and implore Him." The result of such believing prayer will be twofold: First, their hearts will be made sure that they have a compassionate God. Second, God will empower them to help others through their prayers. In this connection Luther makes the astounding assertion that Christ's disciples, reconciled to God and with all their personal needs met, become gods themselves and saviors of others by virtue of their supplications. Having become children of God, they will mediate between God and their neighbors, will serve them, and assist them in becoming followers of Christ and heirs of the kingdom of God.[17]

Luther reminds us that our Father-King is aware of our weaknesses also in prayer. As our gracious and all-knowing Father, he has also acted on our behalf to aid us in our weakness. He has given us an advocate in prayer. This is the Holy Spirit. "The Spirit helps us in our weakness. We do not know what we ought to pray for, but the Spirit himself intercedes for us with groans that words cannot express" (Romans 8:26). It is clear that our weaknesses hinder our prayers. Perhaps we don't know what we should pray for because we doubt the promises of our Father-King. Perhaps we are so ignorant of his perfect will that we offer up ill-advised prayers in faltering tones.

How will our prayers then ring true in the perfect ears of the Father-King so that he will answer us? Scripture tells us we have help. The Holy Spirit lines us up with God and his will. Jesus reminds us that "God is spirit, and his worshipers must worship in spirit and in truth" (John 4:24). To worship in spirit takes the power of the Holy Spirit in our lives. Since prayer is worship, prayer also takes the power of the Holy Spirit in our lives. Thankfully, our Father-King has seen our need and sent his Holy Spirit to us. "Because you are sons, God sent the Spirit of his Son into our hearts, the Spirit who calls out, '*Abba*, Father'" (Galatians 4:6). Lehmann again summarizes Luther's thoughts:

> God certainly hears our prayers even though "we do not know what to pray for" (Romans 8:26). However, instead of asking him for something great, we are too weak and impotent to make large requests. In response to our praying God first nullifies our insignificant petitions for which we prayed in our weakness and instead gives what the Spirit asks for us.[18]

Who would go into court, with all of its legal jargon, on his own if he were offered for free the best lawyer that money could buy? When we approach the Father-King, we will always approach with a certain degree of ignorance of his perfect will. Our prayers will never be what they really could be. The Father-King, however, has put at our disposal an advocate who can take our faltering words and wing them with power to ascend to the heavenly throne.

Should we then approach without him? Rather, let us enlist his help regularly.

Paul encourages all Christians, "Pray in the Spirit on all occasions with all kinds of prayers and requests" (Ephesians 6:18). Just before saying this, Paul had been speaking of the importance of taking the sword of the Spirit, which is the Word of God. Then he continues by urging us to "pray in the Spirit." The connection between the two sentences is the Word of God. We take the sword of the Spirit when we are reading, meditating upon, and using the Word of God. So also, we are praying in the Spirit when our prayers are governed by the Word of God. For the Spirit works in the Word.

Jude gives a similar encouragement to his readers: "Dear friends, build yourselves up in your most holy faith and pray in the Holy Spirit" (Jude 20). These believers are instructed to build up their most holy faith. How is this done? By studying the Word. Faith comes from hearing the message, and faith is continually built up the same way. Jude then connects "pray in the Holy Spirit" with building up our faith. In other words, praying in the Holy Spirit is accomplished by first meditating on God's Word, through which the Holy Spirit takes possession of our intellect, our emotions, and our will and brings them into harmony with his own—which finally then are in tune with those of our Father-King. We have this wonderful advocate to guide us as we speak to the King. Let us not lose the benefit by failing to remain in the Word.

Summary

In the last two chapters, we have explored the essence of prayer. We have seen that it is part of our worship of God. We have seen how it begins with seeking God's favor. We noted the various forms it could take. We discussed those for whom we should pray. Finally, we rejoiced that we have an advocate to help us pray in our human weakness. It is now time for us to discuss some of the practical aspects of prayer. We are coming to the King. Should we stroll into the King's court and flop ourselves down in a chair beside him? Do we stand or sit when in his presence? How should we speak? Is there a special language for prayer, or can we speak any way we like? Questions such as these will be the focus of our next chapter.

7

Common Courtesy—
The Etiquette of Prayer

Proper etiquette shows a relationship of respect

"Don't speak to me in that tone of voice!" How often haven't we said or heard someone else say those words to a child who has been a bit too brazen? The way we speak to others says something about our understanding of our relationship to them. It is children who have gotten too big for their britches and forgotten their proper place who begin to speak to their parents in disrespectful tones. It isn't, however, only the tone of our voices that communicates things about our current state of mind and our attitude toward the person to whom we are speaking. Experts tell us that as much as 65 percent of our communication takes place through nonverbal cues.[19] This includes the way we sit or stand, what we are doing with our hands or our feet, and where we fix our eyes.

We maintain a certain etiquette when we talk to people, dependent upon our relationship with them. Certainly, we always want to show respect. However, we do talk to our friends differently than we would speak to a judge in a courtroom. It is expected there that we use the term "Your Honor" out of deference to the judge's position over us. For a policeman, we might use the title "Officer." If we were granted an audience with a king in ancient times, we would also be expected to follow a certain degree of etiquette. We wouldn't speak to the king lying down, for example. We wouldn't just blurt things out without first being invited to speak. We would be careful about our choice of words. We might even kneel as we come near and bow our heads as a sign of our submission to his authority. All these things would show our relationship and attitude toward this dignitary.

Society and established norms give us guidance on how to speak to various people around us. As we approach the Father-King, Holy Scripture serves as our guide. Following what Scripture says will keep us from creating artificial rules about how we must act before the Lord. Scripture will also keep us from approaching the Lord in ways that would show him disrespect or dishonor.

Posture

To begin with, let's discuss our posture in prayer. As we search the Scriptures, we will find that nowhere does the Lord specify that we must pray in a certain posture—standing, lying, kneeling, sitting, or the like. Therefore, we cannot make a rule and say that when we pray to the Father-King, we must take this or that posture. However, there are some examples in Scripture that might give us some guidance.

Kneeling

In several places in Scripture, we find that those who came to the Lord in prayer did, in fact, kneel before him. Solomon did this during his prayer at the dedication of the new temple in Jerusalem. "When Solomon had finished all these prayers and supplications to the LORD, he rose from before the altar of the LORD, where he had been kneeling with his hands spread out toward heaven" (1 Kings 8:54). Daniel likewise knelt in private to pray to the Lord. "When Daniel learned that the decree had been published, he went home to his upstairs room where the windows opened toward Jerusalem. Three times a day he got down on his knees and prayed, giving thanks to his God, just as he had done before" (6:10).

Perhaps the most outstanding example of this posture is our Lord Jesus himself while he was in the Garden of Gethsemane. Luke 22:41 tells us that Jesus knelt and prayed. Mark 14:35 says that Jesus fell to the ground and prayed, perhaps indicating here that not only did Jesus kneel, but he then bent his body toward the ground so that his face was literally in the dirt. Matthew 26:39 seems to confirm this, for there we are told that Jesus fell with his face to the ground and prayed.

The early Christian church did not cast aside this posture for prayer. Luke tells us in the book of Acts that when Paul was ready to leave Tyre on his way back to Jerusalem at the end of his third missionary journey, the whole group of believers that was sending him off got on their knees together and prayed. "When our time was up, we left and continued on our way. All the disciples and their wives and children accompanied us out of the city, and there on the beach we knelt to pray" (21:5). This was a common practice for Paul, as can be seen in his letter to the Ephesians where he writes, "I kneel before the Father. . . . I pray . . . to him who is able to do immeasurably more than all we ask or imagine" (3:14-20).

This last passage is particularly significant because Paul says that he kneels before *the Father*. Kneeling is a sign of submission and reverence. We may think that since God is our heavenly Father, we may be a bit less formal with him. Yet Paul tells us that he still shows the Father this reverence and respect. Especially in Western culture where respect for our elders and even our parents is not shown readily anymore, the symbolic meaning of kneeling is important to remember. *The Father* is still *the King*. Though our relationship is as close and personal as dear children with their dear father, we still owe and will show our Father the respect of our King.

The survey that this author had sent out had asked the participants whether they ever went to a private place to pray. If they had, they were asked to indicate whether they ever got down on their knees to pray in that private place. Sixty-seven percent of the respondents indicated that they did go to a private place to pray. However, only seven percent of those said that they took the posture of kneeling when they prayed in their private place. On the other hand, 57 percent of all those who filled out the survey indicated that they had knelt while praying at some time. This seems to say that while a majority of us do get down on our knees once in a while in prayer, it is not a common practice.

Certainly, we are not going to assert that we must kneel in prayer. There is, however, good precedence in both the Old and New Testaments to propose that this is a very appropriate posture for prayer. It certainly conveys the proper relationship between us children-servants who pray and the Father-King to whom we pray. It also helps us remember our relationship. Perhaps the examples in Scripture also suggest to us that the posture of kneeling in prayer was more appropriate for some prayers than for others. For example, a person kneeled when he or she had some particular grief or need that he or she earnestly wanted to express to the Lord. This may have been the posture of choice also when confession was due to the Father-King. This, however, as we will see in a moment, cannot be maintained as an absolute.

Standing

Believers in the Scripture also stood when they prayed. In 1 Samuel we read, "As surely as you live, my lord, I am the woman who stood here beside you praying to the LORD" (1:26). These are the words of Hannah to the high priest Eli. In great distress Hannah stood as she prayed to the Lord for the gift of a child. In Nehemiah we read that the contrite people of Israel as a collective body "stood in their places and confessed their sins and the wickedness of their fathers" (9:2). In the New Testament there are any number of instances when Jesus prayed while standing. Jesus even began an instruction of his disciples on one occasion with "When you stand praying . . ." (Mark 11:25).

Interestingly, standing to pray may have had a different significance for the people of the ancient Near East than we today might suspect. A footnote in Kittel's *Theological*

Dictionary of the New Testament explains that according to the Talmud, standing was "the attitude of the slave before his master."[20] This insight may also help us to understand why in many churches today, the congregation commonly rises to pray rather than remains seated. Another possible explanation may be given by Augustine, who lived during the fourth and fifth centuries A.D. In regard to public, or liturgical, prayers, Augustine writes, "On the days which are celebrated after the Lord's Resurrection . . . we pray standing. This symbolizes the Resurrection. Hence at the altar the practice is followed on all Sundays. . . . I do not know whether *standing* during those days and on all Sundays is observed everywhere."[21] On the other hand, Tertullian, who lived during the second and third centuries A.D., indicates that the practice in the early Christian church may first have been to kneel for prayer and then later have shifted to standing. "With regard to kneeling, too, prayer allows a difference in custom because of certain ones . . . who stay off their knees on the Sabbath, an opposing point of view which is just now strongly defending itself in the churches. The Lord will give His grace so that either they will yield, or else maintain their own opinion without giving scandal to others."[22]

It appears that today it is more common for us to stand in private than to kneel. In the survey, among those who go to a private place to pray, 24 percent stood to pray—which is considerably higher than the 7 percent who knelt. Overall, 74 percent of those who were surveyed have prayed at some time and some place by standing. This makes sense, considering that many churches pray with the congregation standing.

Sitting

Scripture only rarely mentions sitting as a posture for prayer. King David "sat before the LORD" and prayed, according to 2 Samuel 7:18. Elijah sat under a broom tree and prayed (1 Kings 19:4). The people of Israel "sat before God" at Bethel, raising their voices to the Lord (Judges 21:2). More commonly, it appears that biblical people either stood or knelt to pray. Compare this to the fact that 51 percent of those who prayed in a private place sat while praying, according to this author's survey. In addition, 81 percent of all respondents have at some time prayed while sitting. Sitting seems to be more the posture of choice for private prayer among American Christians than standing or kneeling.

It seems that in most Christian churches in America, standing is the most common posture for prayer during corporate worship. In Western culture, standing is a sign of respect. By contrast, in some African cultures, sitting is a sign of submission, while standing is a sign of equality between the person speaking and the one listening. Therefore, Christians in some African churches prefer to pray in a seated position to reflect their humble awe of the King. It is worth repeating that there is no biblical mandate for any particular posture in prayer. What is communicated symbolically by posture will depend largely upon culture and tradition.

Lying down

What has been said about sitting might also apply to lying down while we pray. There are no specific references in the Bible to lying down while praying. A few references might suggest that this is happening, but they are very unusual circumstances. For example, Jonah prayed while in the belly of the great fish. It is hard to picture Jonah standing, sitting, or kneeling in the belly of that fish. Perhaps we might say that he prayed while lying down. Two psalm passages also indicate that a person was possibly lying down on a bed while praying. Psalm 6:6 says, "I am worn out from groaning; all night long I flood my bed with weeping and drench my couch with tears." Psalm 63:6 says "On my bed I remember you; I think of you through the watches of the night." The first passage obviously speaks of an extreme situation where the psalmist was in great turmoil of soul. The second passage does not necessarily refer to prayer. It may be that the psalmist was simply thinking about the Lord while lying on his bed and was not praying as such. The point is that lying down doesn't appear to be common or the preferred posture for prayer in the Scriptures.

Based on the survey taken in preparation for this book, it appears that many pray their last prayer of the day while lying in bed. Fifty-four percent of those who indicated that they prayed in a private place said that they prayed most often while lying down. This was the highest percentage of any of the postures used in a private place of prayer. Eighty-two percent of the respondents said that at least once they had prayed while lying down. These percentages suggest that perhaps the private place is our beds at night or in the morning.

Hands

Let's move on, for the moment, to what we do with our hands while we pray. In the survey, only two percent of those who go to a private place to pray raised their hands upward to pray. Just nine percent of all respondents have ever done this anywhere that they have prayed. Yet this is a common way of praying in Scripture. Earlier we looked at the passage that describes how Solomon knelt in prayer at the time of the dedication of the temple (1 Kings 8:54). You might have noticed that he also spread his hands toward heaven in prayer as he knelt. Moses followed this same practice when he prayed for Pharaoh. He told Pharaoh, "'When I have gone out of the city, I will spread out my hands in prayer to the LORD. . . .' Then Moses left Pharaoh and went out of the city. He spread out his hands toward the LORD" (Exodus 9:29,33). A very familiar passage, which we use in our liturgy, expresses this as a very common practice: "May my prayer be set before you like incense; may the lifting up of my hands be like the evening sacrifice" (Psalm 141:2). Paul also mentions this practice when he commands Timothy to teach his congregation to pray: "I want men everywhere to lift up holy hands in prayer, without anger or disputing" (1 Timothy 2:8).

It is noteworthy that even though this common posture for prayer is mentioned often in Scripture, Lutherans do not practice it very much. Christians in certain other denominations do commonly raise their hands in prayer. It seems awkward for us to do this. Perhaps this is an area where Lutherans might rethink their custom and consider a change for a good reason. The reason might be as Kittel suggests, "It is natural that the hands should be lifted up. . . . Since emphasis is laid on the fact that the palms are outstretched, the gesture gives us a position in which gifts may be received from the deity."[23]

On the other hand, perhaps the Lutheran practice of hands down and head down has some basis in Scripture. The parable of the Pharisee and the tax collector is one we have learned from childhood on (Luke 18:9-14). The Pharisee stood in the temple, out in the open, and proudly prayed his self-centered prayer to the Lord. The tax collector moved off into the shadows and hung his head and prayed in deep sorrow and humility. Jesus indicates his approval of what the tax collector did. Perhaps we feel that to raise our hands to the Lord is somewhat proud and presumptuous. Perhaps we feel more comfortable coming to the Lord with our heads hanging low in humble sorrow. The best course might be to practice some of both.

Interestingly, we find no example in Scripture of someone folding his or her hands while praying. Typically, pictures of Jesus in the Garden of Gethsemane show Jesus with his hands folded on a large rock. This is not mentioned in Scripture, nor does it square with the true posture that Jesus took as he knelt and fell on his face. Nevertheless, we commonly teach our children to fold their hands while they pray. Perhaps the thinking is that our folded hands are less likely to distract us by doing something else while we pray. Eighty-five percent of those surveyed said that they have folded their hands at some time when praying. Fifty-six percent of those surveyed who go to a private place fold their hands regularly. This is a good custom. It is, however, only a custom. Scripture does not insist that our hands be folded to pray.

Head

Scripture does not insist that our heads be bowed when we pray. Just as believers often lifted up their hands in prayer, so also they often lifted up their heads. A notable exception is the tax collector whom we have mentioned. His situation, however, seemed to dictate a different posture. On more than one occasion when Jesus prayed, we are told that he looked up. He did this while praying at the tomb of Lazarus (John 11:41), for example. As he began his High Priestly Prayer in John chapter 17, we are told, Jesus "looked toward heaven and prayed" (verse 1). In the survey this author conducted, only 11 percent of those who pray in a private place raise their heads on a regular basis when they pray. Only 47 percent of all those who said they pray had ever raised their heads when they prayed. As already mentioned, perhaps this has something to do with our view of what lifting our heads up says to the Father-King.

Concluding observations

As we close this chapter on the etiquette of prayer, allow this author a few concluding observations. Many Christians go to sleep at night with a prayer on their lips. What better way could there be to end the day than to be praying to our Father-King for his blessings and peace before we sleep? The problem we have is that we often fall asleep while saying that prayer—due mainly to our posture. It is all too easy for our weak flesh to doze off while lying in our beds rather than to tend to our prayers. While falling asleep with a prayer on our lips or in our hearts is not all bad, at the same time we have to wonder what that says to our Father-King. Remember, we are speaking to him. How would you feel if someone fell asleep in the middle of a conversation with you?

Another danger is that these "dozing" prayers might also be our only prayers. If this is the case, it appears from Scripture that we may want to rethink our practice. The Father-King deserves more respect and honor from us when he grants us this audience than to give him only the few tired minutes we have before bedtime. Perhaps "better time" prayers need to replace or at least supplement our bedtime prayers. In other words, we need to talk to the Lord when we can really focus and have a serious conversation with him. This is in regard to our private prayers, of course.

The prayers we pray in church by necessity will not be spoken lying down. The issue for us then is more along the line of sitting, standing, or kneeling, as well as hands folded or hands raised. While these are not directives from Scripture, let's consider what the early Christian church did. Tertullian, a church father from North Africa, commented about what his congregation members did with their hands: "In our case, not only do we raise them, we even spread them out, and, imitating the Passion of our Lord, we confess Christ as we pray."[24] At Tertullian's time it was common to kneel for prayer, although standing was becoming an alternative. Clement of Rome, writing in the first century of the Christian church, exhorted, "Let us come before Him, then, in sanctity of soul, lifting pure and undefiled hands to Him."[25] It appears from this comment that the common practice for his congregation members was to raise their collective hands in prayer. This did not, however, exclude the possibility of other postures. In another place he wrote, "Let us quickly remove this, then, and let us fall down before the Lord and supplicate Him with tears that He may become merciful and be reconciled to us."[26] The situation at the time of this latter quote was obviously different from that which existed when Clement wrote the words found in the first quote.

The conclusion this leads to is that it is best if our posture in prayer reflects the content of our prayers. Some situations may call for a more subdued posture, with head down and hands low, reflecting the attitude of our hearts. Other situations may call for a posture in which our heads are up and our hands are raised wide over our heads. Certainly, it would seem to be out of character to bow our heads and lower our hands when our hearts are singing. Occasions of praise, thanksgiving, and adoration for the goodness of our Father-King seem to beg for heads and hands uplifted to the Glorious One on his throne.

Above all, we must keep in mind that the posture of prayer is an adiaphoron, something neither commanded by God nor forbidden by him. So we dare not condemn those who pray in postures different from ours. Nor dare we make rules about the only proper way to pray. Nevertheless, we need to be aware that what our posture says to the Father-King does make a difference. In our posture, let us remember to *whom* we are praying.

8

More Etiquette: Language and Location

No special vocabulary for prayer

One of the reasons often given by those who aren't actively praying is that they don't know how to pray. They don't know what words to speak. They feel that there is a certain vocabulary for prayer, which they first have to learn in order to pray. The purpose of this book is to encourage prayers to the Father-King. At the same time, this book also leads us to seek guidance from Scripture for our prayers so that we do not offend the Father-King with our prayers. This is true also of the words we use.

Jesus, the one who gained us an audience with the King, gives guidance about what we should say to the

King. "When you pray, do not keep on babbling like pagans, for they think they will be heard because of their many words" (Matthew 6:7). Just saying words is not what the King wants from us when we come into his presence. The pagans believed that the more words they said, the better chance they had of receiving what they wanted. The idea was that the amount of words gained favor. Christians find themselves in a completely different situation. Our prayers already have the favor of our King because of the merits of his Son, Jesus Christ. We do not need to pray lots of words to be heard. We need only to come in the name of the Savior. (We will say more on this subject in a later chapter.)

There is no special language for prayer that is different from the language we use to speak to one another. In public our language might be a bit more formal. In private, where we pour out our hearts to our Father-King, our prayers might be less formal. Certainly, language that is disrespectful or vulgar will not be part of our prayers. Other than that, Scripture does not restrict the words we use to pray. Luther serves as a fine model for us in his approach to prayer:

> Referring to his own way of praying, Luther stated that in praying he did not adhere rigidly to a given pattern. He did not cling slavishly to the exact words of a prayer, but expressed himself in a certain way on one day and in another way on the following day, depending on his personal circumstances. In general, however, he kept before him some basic thoughts and guidelines.[27]

Prayer books or prayers we make up?

Is it better to pray prayers that we find in a prayer book, or is it better to pray in our own words? The answer is that neither is necessarily better or worse. There may be times for both. The Old Testament believers had many prayers that were written down for them to use. This was the purpose of the book of Psalms. The psalms weren't written just for us to see how the people prayed back then. The psalms, many of which are prayers, were written for the people of Israel to use in worship. It was anticipated that the people would pray these prewritten prayers. This was often done in congregational worship settings. Praying the psalms allowed the congregation members to join together with one voice and lift their prayers to the Lord in heaven. We do something similar when we use prayers or psalms out of our hymnals in our worship services. These allow us to pray together as a body.

Jesus also gave us some specific words that we can use to speak to our Father-King. These words, which we know as the Lord's Prayer, are not many in number. Their language is simple and straightforward. We can pray these words privately or as a congregation. They comprise a simple way to pray. Yet Jesus does not say that these are the only words we should pray. He says, "This, then, is *how* you should pray: . . ." (Matthew 6:9). He is giving us a pattern for our prayers.

The early Christians recognized that prayers could be what are called *ex corde* prayers. This simply means "from the heart." One needs only to read through the book of Acts to see how many different occasions prompted different prayers from the early believers. They had Jesus' pattern, yet they felt the Christian freedom to speak to God in words that expressed whatever need or praise or confession they had at that moment.

So it is with us. We can pray whatever words express our thanks or need at that moment. We might simply make up our own prayers. Or there may be times when prayers don't come to us. In those moments, perhaps we may want to pray the Lord's Prayer. Or perhaps we might benefit from prayers that other believers have written which capture the thoughts we would like to speak to our Father-King.

Out loud or in the heart?

Another issue that warrants our consideration is whether to pray out loud or only in our hearts. In the survey to which we have referred, 78 percent of those who pray in a private place indicated that they "say" their prayers silently. Twenty-one percent indicated that they speak them out loud. Another 21 percent (at times respondents chose more than one option, indicating that they didn't always pray the same way) said they sometimes prayed by moving their lips without making any audible sounds. Does the Scripture give any indication regarding praying out loud or silently?

Perhaps the prayer of Hannah is fairly familiar to us (1 Samuel 1:9-16). The Scripture notes that Eli reprimanded Hannah after observing that she was moving her lips in prayer but was making no sounds. Eli the priest believed that she was drunk and therefore out of line in offering a prayer to the Lord. Hannah defended herself and explained that she was in such anguish of heart that as she prayed, her lips moved without sound. From this it appears that it was unusual to pray without making sounds, otherwise it would not have drawn the attention of Eli.

Scripture, however, gives no indication that all prayers *must* be spoken out loud. Certainly, corporate prayers will be spoken out loud. But privately, Christians may communicate with God in their thoughts and minds because God knows what we are thinking at all times (see Matthew 12:25). David could say about the Lord, "You perceive my thoughts from afar. Before a word is on my tongue you know it completely, O LORD" (Psalm 139:2,4).

There are some benefits to praying out loud over only praying in our hearts. Obviously, when praying with other Christians, vocalization helps us harmonize our thoughts and bring a uniform prayer from the congregation to the Lord. Privately too, there are benefits. Praying out loud in private keeps us aware of the reality of our prayers. Praying isn't just a mental exercise that picks up our spirits simply by going through a process. Prayer is speaking to the King. If we were sitting in a room when someone walked in and we wanted to ask him a question or invite him to sit down, we wouldn't just think those things; we would say them to him. Granted, God knows our hearts and our minds. Still, the reality that we are indeed speaking to God and that he is hearing us is increased when we verbalize our prayers. Speaking them out loud also makes it less likely that our minds will wander or drift off into sleep.

Praying "continually"

Another question—similar to, How should we speak to our Father-King?—is, How often should we pray? We read earlier that Daniel knelt in prayer three times a day (Daniel 6:10). Frequently, we read about Jesus going off to a quiet place to pray (Matthew 14:23; Luke 5:16; 6:12; 9:28; Mark 1:35). We also note that Jesus prayed prior to some of his miracles (Matthew 14:19; John 11:41,42). He prayed with his disciples on the night he was betrayed (Matthew 26:39-44). He prayed on the cross (Luke 23:34). Jesus prayed often. The apostle Paul instructed the believers in Thessalonica to "pray continually"

(1 Thessalonians 5:17). It should be obvious that Paul cannot mean that we should be engaged in saying the Lord's Prayer or some other prayer every waking moment of every day. Paul is rather urging Christians to pray frequently. Every opportunity to talk with the Father-King should be seized by his children-subjects.

In his letter to the Christians at Rome, Paul pens this encouragement: "Be joyful in hope, patient in affliction, faithful in prayer" (Romans 12:12). Being faithful in prayer means that we don't just pray when the world is about to fall apart. It means that we regularly speak to our Father-King. It means that we don't let other things distract us and infringe upon our time to pray. How often we pray is really related to how often we listen to the Father-King speak and how close our relationship with him has grown. The closer we are to him, the more we are going to want to talk with him.

Frequent prayers often also make us better praying Christians. In his book *The Practice of Prayer*, Oscar Feucht offers this thoughtful advice:

> Ignace Jan Paderewski became the celebrated pianist because in his youth he practiced three hours each morning and again three hours every afternoon. Throughout his brilliant career he kept up rigorous schedules of daily practice. It is said that if he missed a single day, he noticed it; if he missed two days, the critics noticed it; and if he missed three days, the public noticed it. When we do not keep up the daily keyboard exercises, we lose our skills in playing. It is the same with prayer.[28]

Prayer is part of our Christian sanctification, that is, our living as a Christian. Christians grow in sanctification. They become better at living as Christians. So we also grow in prayer. We become better at praying the more we practice.

One location for prayer is public worship

The last question to answer in this chapter is, Where will we practice our prayer?

Certainly, one place is with other Christians in public worship. One purpose for gathering together regularly with Christians for worship is to bring our prayers collectively to God. Worship is a two-way activity. God comes to us in Word and sacrament. We also come to him with our prayers and praise. During our busy weeks, it is good to know that we have this time set aside every week, scheduled for God's Word and prayer.

The location for these joint prayers, however, should always be with believers who share with us the same confession of faith in the teachings of God's Word. Praying with other people is an act of Christian fellowship. God's Word instructs us not to share in Christian fellowship with people who hold to false teachings (Romans 16:17; Titus 3:10).

Experienced worshipers find that the prayers of public worship also enrich their private prayers. The prayers we hear and join in at church serve as a pattern for us. They teach us what to pray for, and they give us a working vocabulary for prayer.

Location for personal prayers

What about our personal prayers? Is location important? Since we are to pray frequently—"continually," according to Paul—do we need to be in a certain location in order to do this? If we were to continue the illustration of an earthly king at this point, we could only pray if we were in his throne room. This would be the only place he could hear us. Not so with our heavenly King. His ability to hear our prayers is not limited by our location. It's not so important where we are, but where he is. The Scripture tells us that our Father-King is everywhere. His throne and dominion fill all the earth. No matter where we are, he is there. So wherever we are is a place where we can pray to the King. In this sense, location is not at all an issue.

In another sense, location is an issue. Location might be an issue for us when we ask the question, Is it appropriate for us to pray in any place? Or to put it another way, Should I pray my prayers publicly, where everyone can see me, or in private, where no one else can witness them? The answer to this question has much to do with our inner motive for praying. Jesus once spoke about a Pharisee and a tax collector who went to the temple to pray. The Pharisee stood up in the middle of the temple courtyard where everyone could see him pray. He wanted *others* to notice that he was praying. He was not so concerned that God was listening. Jesus warns his disciples about this practice of the Pharisees when he told them that some like to stand in the synagogues and on street corners to be seen by people. Then Jesus instructed them about where to pray: "But when you pray, go into your room, close the door and pray to your Father, who is unseen. Then your Father, who sees what is done in secret, will reward you" (Matthew 6:6). In the context it is clear that Jesus is not telling his disciples that they are never to utter a prayer when someone else might see or hear them praying. Rather, the point is that our prayers are not to be shows for people to see, but heartfelt conversations with God. For this reason even Jesus often prayed in private, as the gospel of Luke records: "Jesus often withdrew to lonely places and prayed" (5:16).

On the other hand, we dare not be ashamed to let others see us pray, as long as the motive isn't to draw attention to ourselves and our praying. Jesus wasn't ashamed to pray in public when he gave thanks for food before feeding the five thousand (Matthew 14:19). Nor was he ashamed to pray in public when he prayed before raising Lazarus from the dead (John 11:41,42). Likewise, on the cross Jesus publicly uttered prayers for the soldiers who crucified him (Luke 23:34) and even for himself (Matthew 27:46).

The apostle Paul followed in the footsteps of his Master. When he was jailed in Philippi, Paul did not hesitate to pray, even though others could hear him (Acts 16:25). When he was leaving Tyre, he was not afraid to kneel down with the whole congregation right on the beach and offer a prayer to the Lord (Acts 21:5). These certainly weren't private places. Yet Paul kept the principle that Jesus gave. Prayers are not to be said to gain the praise of people; they are to be spoken to the Lord unashamedly whenever we have a need.

With this in mind, it certainly is not violating Jesus' words to bow our heads in a restaurant and offer a prayer before we eat our meal. We don't pray to draw attention to ourselves as if to say, "Hey, everyone, look what a good person I am. I'm going to pray over my food before I eat it now!" Rather, we pray out of sincere gratitude for the gift of food that the Lord has given us—whether at home or in a restaurant. Indeed, if we do *not* pray because we are afraid of people noticing and thinking, "Hey, there's one of those religious fanatics," then we are really denying Christ and being ashamed of him. God forbid that we are ashamed of being Christians.

Likewise, other than in a worship service, we might pray in the presence of others at the scene of an accident as we ask the Lord to be with the victims. Or perhaps we might pray in a hospital room with a sick relative or family member. There isn't going to be much privacy there. Yet we will pray despite who may hear us simply because this is what God's children do when they have a need. They come to God and talk to him about it. They ask him for his help. They praise him for his goodness and aid.

Most often, however, we will want to seek out a private place to pray, as Jesus instructed his disciples. For one thing, this allows us to carry on our conversation with our Father-King with the least number of distractions. It should go without saying that this private place should not be disturbed by any TV or radio or other things that are under our control. Our private place might be a bedroom, office, car, or somewhere outdoors. The important thing is that it is a place we can get to daily and have a few moments when others won't bother us there. In some cases this might mean asking others not to disturb us for a while. This, of course, must be done in such a way that we are not flaunting our praying.

In the survey this author conducted, only 32 percent of those who responded indicated that they take time daily to go to a private place to speak with the Lord. While a private place is not the only place to pray, and while Jesus had a certain context in mind when giving his disciples this instruction, yet one is surprised that we don't follow Jesus' instruction a bit more. Perhaps there is room for improvement here. Do we not go to a private place because it takes too much effort? because we are too busy? because we don't think it is that important? because we don't see the need? Then perhaps we need to review the first chapters of this book again and remember what a blessed privilege prayer is. What greater happiness could there be each day than to have a few moments to talk heart to heart with the Father-King, who dotes on us as his dearly loved children? Nothing could bring us greater blessings than those minutes in our private place of prayer.

This is especially true as we come to realize what we can ask of our Father-King. This we will see in our next chapter.

9

An Open Invitation from the King

The King has the power to give anything

Can you imagine being summoned to the palace of the most powerful ruler in the world and being told that you can ask for anything you would like and it will be yours? Absolutely anything! Can you imagine being young Solomon when he had just ascended the throne of Israel, and the Lord came to him and told him to ask for anything he wanted and it would be his? Kings have this kind of authority. Since there is no one greater in the kingdom than the king, he has the right to grant whatever he wants to whomever he wants. Even some lesser kings have such authority.

King Herod, though he wasn't equal to the caesar in Rome, had authority in his little area of the world. So when Herodias, the daughter of Herod's wife, pleased Herod with her dancing, Herod promised her anything she wanted, up to half of his kingdom. Essentially, he offered her the key to the wealth of his kingdom. Unfortunately, the Bible relates to us that upon the counsel of her mother, she made the darkest of requests: the head of John the Baptist (Mark 6:22-25). But the point is that a king has the power, the right, and the authority to give whatever he wants to those who are pleasing to him. He can open up to them the treasuries of his kingdom.

"Whatever you ask in my name"

Through his Son, Jesus, the Father-King opens up the treasuries of his kingdom to us. This is what Jesus' word *whatever* means. Jesus told his followers, "If you believe, you will receive *whatever* you ask for in prayer" (Matthew 21:22). In the context, "if you believe" does not only refer to faith in Jesus. It refers here primarily to believing in God's ability to give us whatever we ask. It refers to asking without any doubt of receiving what we ask. This promise is perhaps more clearly stated in Mark's parallel account, where Jesus says, "I tell you, whatever you ask for in prayer, believe that you have received it, and it will be yours" (11:24). What Jesus is trying to impress upon us is that through his merits as our Savior, we have been connected to the unbelievable power and ability of our Father-King. There is nothing he cannot do. Nor is there anything good that he does not want to do for those who are his children by faith in Jesus.

There is a voice in us that immediately questions whether Jesus really means what he says here: Jesus can't possibly mean *whatever*, even though he says "whatever." Is God really going to give us anything we choose to ask from him? The answer is a resounding "Yes!" Jesus' words are plain. At this point, some will remind us of the passage in John's first letter that says, "This is the confidence we have in approaching God: that if we ask anything according to his will, he hears us. And if we know that he hears us—whatever we ask—we know that we have what we asked of him" (5:14,15). This passage seems to inject some doubt into Jesus' "whatever"—whatever, *if* it agrees with God's will. Yet agreeing with God's will does not create doubt about our receiving what we ask; rather, John says it gives us greater assurance. For when we ask according to God's will, then we know with absolute certainty that he hears us. And since he hears us, we know that "what we asked of him" we will receive.

How and when do we pray "according to his will"? Perhaps the best example of this is found in the Garden of Gethsemane the night before Jesus was crucified. There our Savior himself poured out his heart and soul to his Father in heaven. "Going a little farther, he fell to the ground and prayed that if possible the hour might pass from him. '*Abba*, Father,' he said, 'everything is possible for you. Take this cup from me. Yet not what I will, but what you will'" (Mark 14:35,36). Notice that Jesus didn't doubt that his Father in heaven could do what he asked. He asked him for "whatever." He had every confidence that he would receive what he asked. Yet what he asked was not only that the Father would take the cup of suffering away from him. He asked that the Father would do what was in accord with the Father's will. A few hours later it became clear that the Father was not going to take the cup of suffering away from Jesus. Yet in one sense, the Father still gave Jesus what Jesus asked for, because the Father did what was in keeping with his will. It was not his will to remove the cup, but that

Jesus would suffer for our salvation. And this was what Jesus asked for.

Jesus always asked the right thing because he was perfect. The apostle Paul reminds us in Romans 8:26 that "we do not know what we ought to pray for" at times. In other words, we don't always know what God's will is. It is good to remind ourselves that our personal desires expressed in prayer are not always what God desires for us. For us there will always be a battle going on within us between our old, sinful nature and our new self, which lives in us by the power of the Holy Spirit. Sometimes our sinful nature influences our thinking and distracts us from first seeking the kingdom of God. Because of our sinful nature, we do not always fully grasp the will of God, and we can't see clearly what the will of our Father is. Also, sometimes the Father in heaven has simply not revealed his will to us regarding certain details of our lives, that we might know it and pray according to it. According to his human nature during his state of humiliation, Jesus also did not always know the exact method of accomplishing God's will. For this reason he sought to know his Father's will in prayer—such as at Gethsemane.

Certainly, some requests we know to be God's will. With spiritual blessings like the forgiveness of sins and a stronger faith, we know for sure that they are in keeping with the Lord's will. So we don't pray, "Forgive my sins, if it is your will." We ask for eternal life and God's spiritual blessings without any qualifications. But when we pray for specific temporal blessings for which we don't have a direct promise from God, we always pray "not my will be done but yours," as Jesus did. This prevents us from ever praying for anything that is not according to God's will. We can pray for whatever we think we need or we think is best.

Finally, however, we need to realize that we may not be privy to the wisdom of God on the matter. Our way may not be best. So we offer our "suggestion" and then allow God to do what is best. This is not always easy to practice. Perhaps the following example is helpful. "Some people tend to think of prayer as a rope attaching a huge ship to a little boat. They are the boat, and the big ship is God's will. They think the rope of prayer is to be used to pull the big ship alongside their little boat. This is against all natural laws, just as it is against all spiritual laws to say, 'Not Thy will but mine be done!'"[29]

The "whatever" of Jesus must always be understood in the context of the new self in us. The new self wants only what God wants. The new self is not going to ask for something that is contrary to God's will. Essentially, it wants God's will to become our will. This is why we pray, "not my will, but yours be done." This is not saying to God, "Here is what I want Lord. I think this is the way it should be done, but I guess you'll do it your way anyway so I might as well concede to you." Rather, it is to say, "Lord, this is the best I can figure out with my limited knowledge and faith. You are much wiser and far more powerful than I can imagine. Do what you know is really best. Then I will make that my will and gladly request it instead!" With this kind of prayer on our lips, we can never fail to receive whatever we ask, since it is whatever God wants.

More than we can imagine

What increases our amazement at this "whatever" of Jesus is that we don't even begin to ask what we might from our Father-King. The apostle Paul told the Ephesian Christians to give glory to God, "who is able to do immeasurably more than all we ask or imagine, according to his power that is at work within us" (3:20). Sometimes we think maybe we are being too bold and asking God for too much. Paul tells us that most of the time we are insulting his greatness by asking for far less than he could give us. This is a good time for us to go back to the beginning of this book and remember *to whom* we are praying. He is not some earthly king who, though great, still has only limited resources and power. Our audience is before the King of the universe, who has all things in heaven and earth at his beck and command. As the Bible so often reminds us, nothing is impossible for him (Matthew 19:26; Luke 1:37).

John Newton told the story of a man who asked Alexander the Great to give him a huge sum of money in exchange for his daughter's hand in marriage. The ruler consented and told the man to request of the treasurer whatever he wanted. So he went and asked for an enormous amount. The keeper of the funds was startled and said he couldn't give him that much without a direct order. Going to Alexander, the treasurer argued that even a small fraction of the money requested would more than serve the purpose. "No," replied Alexander, "let him have it all. I like that fellow. He does me honor. He treats me like a king and proves by what he asks that he believes me to be both rich and generous."[30] So it is that we truly honor our Father-King when we come to him with big, bold prayers rather than tiny, timid prayers of little trust in his goodness and power. This same John Newton is the author of a well-known hymn that contains these words: "You are coming to a king—large petitions with you bring, for his grace and pow'r are such, none can ever ask too much."[31]

So often the truth of what God's Word tells us is grasped more readily by a young child than by those of us who are more mature. Consider how completely the little girl in this story from Dr. Helen Roseveare, a missionary to the Belgian Congo (Zaire today), shows her trust in Jesus' "whatever."

> A mother at our mission station died after giving birth to a premature baby. We tried to improvise an incubator to keep the infant alive, but the only hot water bottle we had was beyond repair. So during devotions that morning we asked the children to pray for the baby and for her little sister who was now an orphan. One of the girls responded, "Dear God, please send a hot water bottle today. Tomorrow will be too late because by then the baby will be dead. And dear Lord, send a doll for the sister so she won't feel so lonely." That afternoon a large parcel arrived from England. Eagerly the children watched as we opened it. Much to their surprise, under some clothing was a hot water bottle! Immediately the girl who had prayed so earnestly started to delve deeper, exclaiming, "If God sent that, I'm sure He also sent a doll." And she was right! The Heavenly Father knew in advance of the child's sincere requests, and 5 months before, He had led a ladies group to include both of those specific articles.[32]

It is only when we doubt our Father-King's power and love that we fail to ask for the blessings that he is so willing to give us.

"Whatever" is always "in Jesus' name"

What makes the Father-King so willing to answer our prayers is the salvation won for us by Jesus Christ. This is the reason our prayers must be offered in Jesus' name, as Scripture teaches us in many places. It is necessary, however, that we understand what it means to pray "in Jesus' name."

Some believe that praying "in Jesus' name" means that every prayer we pray must end with the words "In Jesus' name I pray. Amen." If that is the case, then most of the prayers that are recorded in the New Testament were not prayed properly, for they do not end with this phrase. It is not that this is a bad thing to do. There is value in reminding ourselves whenever we pray that we come "in Jesus' name." However, just saying the words "in Jesus' name" at the end of our prayers is not what Jesus meant.

To do something in someone's name can have several meanings. For one thing, having someone's name can indicate ownership or belonging. We have our parents' name because we belong to their family. Having someone's name or operating under someone's name can also mean that we have that person's authority. If one of our diplomats does something in the name of the United States of America, it means that the authority of this country is behind the diplomat. Finally, a person's name is that person's reputation. A name often brings to mind what that person has done or who that person is. For example, if someone were to say the name Joel Petermann, you probably wouldn't be impressed. If someone mentions the name Abraham Lincoln, on the other hand, a sea of thoughts and events would come flooding into your mind.

So when we are told by Jesus to pray "in his name," it means several things for us. First, it means that as we march into the throne room of the King, we go as those who belong to his family. We are not foreigners or servants, but children of the King with the same rights of sonship as Jesus himself enjoys. Second, we march in with the authority of Jesus. He gives us the right to come and ask for things from the King. Jesus was never turned away by his Father when he prayed to him. So also we will never be turned away. Third, we march into the throne room of the King because of what Jesus has done for us. By faith his perfect obedience is ours. His innocent death paid for our sins and makes us acceptable to the King. His resurrection from the dead guarantees our status as children of God and as favored subjects of the kingdom. Finally, when we pray "in Jesus' name," we are praying on the basis of who Jesus is now. He is himself the King of kings and Lord of lords. The King has conveyed to him the throne forever and conveyed all authority to him to grant our wishes. This is what it means to pray "in Jesus' name."

Perhaps the most notable passage in which Jesus instructs us to pray in his name is found in the gospel of John. There Jesus says, "I tell you the truth, my Father will give you whatever you ask in my name. Until now you have not asked for anything in my name. Ask and you will receive, and your joy will be complete" (16:23,24). Unquestionably, something was changing in the way God's people would come to him in prayer. The Old Testament believers had prayed and were heard by God when they prayed according to his promises. Now the fulfillment of those promises had come. Now the Messiah was here. Soon Jesus would pay the price for sin with his blood so that Christians would have complete access to all of God's blessings. It was time for God's people to pray "in Jesus' name." To pray in Jesus' name is to pray with trust in him and with faith in the message of the cross.

Perhaps an illustration can help us to understand the significance of praying in Jesus' name. Even in our human affairs, there is influence in having or going in someone's name. Jill Briscoe relates the following experience:

> Not long ago I had to have some tests at the hospital. My doctor gave me a note, which I carefully clutched to myself as I approached the gate. In his name I announced my arrival. There was no way I could obtain my confer-

ence with the surgeon without that note signed by my doctor's own hand. I was then instructed to follow a yellow line on the floor that would eventually lead me to the inner office of the specialist who would listen to my problem, diagnose the disease, and prescribe a remedy. I would never have tried to find my own way or take an unauthorized route. Neither did I think of throwing away the name of my doctor who sent me to the surgeon, with all of his authority behind that interview. I was in a different world. The medical world was totally strange and unfamiliar, and who was I to know better than the principalities who ruled that sphere? Following the instructions carefully, I arrived in front of the big man himself. He read my doctor's note, smiled, and gently began to ask me many questions. I was so scared and nervous. If only my doctor was there to be with me and explain my case. Suddenly the door opened and there he was! Knowing my justified fear, he had come himself to be with me.[33]

So it is for us. Jesus has given us his name to carry with us wherever we go. It is his name that has gained entrance for us into the throne room of the King. It is his name that gains us an audience. It is his name that gives us the right to make our requests and to be heard. His name is like an electronic key-card that opens to us the gates of heaven. The best part, however, is that even as we depend on his name with still shaky hands, he is with us, standing by our side and seeing to it that for his sake our requests are honored. Then, as he promises, our joy will be complete.

"Whatever" means God is omnipotent

Luther clearly grasped the full implications of praying in Jesus' name and the "whatever" of Jesus' promise: "True prayer is omnipotent, as our Lord says: 'For everyone who asks receives, etc.'"[34] We learn in catechism class that only God is omnipotent. Yet Luther declares our prayers to be omnipotent. Ultimately, they are. For through faith in Jesus and in his name, we have the promise of the Father-King to grant us whatever we ask. That puts the Father-King's power in our hands, so to speak. It also puts us in alignment with his will.

> The free use of the name of another is always the token of great confidence, of close union. He who gives his name to another stands aside, to let that other act for him; he who takes the name of another gives up his own as of no value. When I go in the name of another, I deny myself, I take not only his name, but himself and what he is, instead of myself and what I am.[35]

This last statement reminds us of the purpose for which Jesus gives us such great promises regarding prayer. We are to ask great things and accomplish great things through prayer because this will glorify our Father-King. "I tell you the truth, anyone who has faith in me will do what I have been doing. He will do even greater things than these, because I am going to the Father. And I will do whatever you ask in my name, so that the Son may bring glory to the Father. You may ask me for anything in my name, and I will do it" (John 14:12-14). Jesus lived to glorify his Father in heaven. His prayers also asked things that would give glory to his Father in heaven. So we who are made new in Christ, who die to self and live for Christ, will be living to glorify our Father-King. Our true prayers spoken in Jesus' name will likewise bring that glory to the Father in heaven, which both Jesus and we desire.

A caution is in order about saying the words "in Jesus' name." When we do say those words frequently, both in our private prayers and also in our public worship services, there is the danger that we begin to say them without thinking. Then the phrase becomes a mechanical thing we do without involving our hearts and minds. Or it may become superstitious, as if those words themselves have magical power to accomplish something. These words in and of themselves do not make a prayer a true prayer.

Pray with confidence

When we do pray true prayers in Jesus' name, however, then we can pray with absolute confidence that the Father-King will hear our prayers. Hebrews 4:14-16 says,

> Since we have a great high priest who has gone through the heavens, Jesus the Son of God, let us hold firmly to the faith we profess. For we do not have a high priest who is unable to sympathize with our weaknesses, but we have one who has been tempted in every way, just as we are—yet was without sin. Let us then approach the throne of grace with confidence, so that we may receive mercy and find grace to help us in our time of need.

We can have confidence because we have a High Priest in heaven, Jesus, who understands what we are going through and who sympathizes with us.

This is the attitude we want to learn to have in prayer. James warns us about the opposite of confident prayers, namely, doubt-filled prayers. "If any of you lacks wisdom, he should ask God, who gives generously to all without finding fault, and it will be given to him. But when he asks, he must believe and not doubt, because he who doubts is like a wave of the sea, blown and tossed by the wind. That man should not think he will receive anything from the Lord" (James 1:5-7). At the heart of such confident prayers is faith in Jesus. Only people who know that

God is at peace with them and is pleased to give them the kingdom can pray with such confidence. Likewise, they must believe firmly in the words and promises of God. Our senses will cause us to doubt, for they often contradict the promises of God. An example would be the time when Peter walked on water on the Sea of Galilee (Matthew 14:28-31). As long as Peter trusted Jesus' words, he could walk. When he looked at the waves coming, he began to believe his senses rather than Jesus' words, and he began to sink. So it is with us in prayer. When we rely only on God's Word and promises, we can be absolutely sure that we will have what we ask for the moment we pray for it. An anecdote is told of a person who immediately followed a prayer of request with a prayer of thanksgiving for what he had just prayed. This was because he was sure he would receive it.

Examples of such confident prayer are numerous in Scripture. Abraham showed such confidence when he pleaded with the Lord to spare Sodom and Gomorrah (Genesis 18:22-32). He knew that the Lord who had revealed himself as just and righteous would not act unjustly toward this city and destroy it if there were a few righteous people there. Boldly, Abraham whittled the number down from 50 to 10. Another example would be Jacob wrestling with the Lord until daybreak at the Jabbok River (Genesis 32:24-30). Jacob held on to the Lord and boldly asserted, "I will not let you go unless you bless me" (verse 26). A third example would be the Canaanite woman who would not give up on her request even after Jesus called the Gentiles, including her, "dogs" (Matthew 15:26). Despite being rebuffed, she continued to come to Jesus again and again, believing that he would grant her what she wanted. None of these believers were wishy-washy. The winds of doubt may have blown around them, but their anchors held in the words and promises of God.

In his characteristic way, Luther minces no words as he gives us some thoughts to ponder regarding praying without doubt or fear.

> You must learn to call. Do not sit by yourself or lie on a couch, hanging and shaking your head. Do not destroy yourself with your own thoughts by worrying. Do not strive and struggle to free yourself, and do not brood on your wretchedness, suffering, and misery. Say to yourself: "Come on, you lazy bum; down on your knees, and lift your eyes and hands toward heaven!" Read a psalm or the Our Father, call on God, and tearfully lay your troubles before Him. . . . Here you learn that praying, reciting your troubles, and lifting up your hands are sacrifices most pleasing to God. It is His desire and will that you lay your troubles before Him. He does not want you to multiply your troubles by burdening and torturing yourself. He wants you to be too weak to bear and overcome such troubles; He wants you to grow strong in Him. By His strength He is glorified in you.[36]

Pray with persistence

Together with confident praying comes another important aspect of prayer, which is persistence. Jesus himself illustrated this for us when he told the parable of the persistent widow (Luke 18:1-8). In this parable a certain widow is being plagued by an adversary. She goes to court and asks the judge for an injunction to stop her enemy from pestering her. The judge, who really doesn't care about God or people at all, refuses to do anything to help her. The widow, however, is persistent. She returns again and again until, finally, the judge, admitting that he really doesn't care about her, nevertheless grants her request because she just won't leave him alone otherwise. Jesus then applies this to our prayers to the Father in heaven. The point is to be persistent. One huge difference exists between the judge and our Father in heaven, however. The judge listened only because he didn't want to be bothered anymore. Our Father in heaven wants to be bothered. He loves us and desires to help us. He is going to grant justice to his people who call upon him persistently.

Jesus gives another illustration regarding bold persistence in Luke chapter 11. It follows immediately after Jesus had been asked by his disciples to teach them how to pray. First Jesus taught them the Lord's Prayer. Then he said to them,

> Suppose one of you has a friend, and he goes to him at midnight and says, "Friend, lend me three loaves of bread, because a friend of mine on a journey has come to me, and I have nothing to set before him." Then the one inside answers, "Don't bother me. The door is already locked, and my children are with me in bed. I can't get up and give you anything." I tell you, though he will not get up and give him the bread because he is his friend, yet because of the man's boldness he will get up and give him as much as he needs. So I say to you: Ask and it will be given to you; seek and you will find; knock and the door will be opened to you. For everyone who asks receives; he who seeks finds; and to him who knocks, the door will be opened. (verses 5-10)

Note that the man who was in bed does *not* help his neighbor because he is his friend. Note that the man in bed initially answers no to the request. It is the other man's persistence that finally gets results. So Jesus wants us also to be persistent—and this before our Father-King, who, unlike the man in bed, is eager to help us and answer our prayers.

Jesus spells out the point for us in the second to last sentence of this text. The NIV translation, unfortunately, does not bring out the full sense of what Jesus is saying. The present tense might be better translated like this: "Keep on asking . . . ; keep on seeking . . . ; keep on knocking." The continuous and persistent activity of prayer is what Jesus is encouraging. Likewise, the words that follow these commands indicate a characteristic activity: "those who are characterized by asking will receive," and so on. Jesus wants us to do more than pray about something once and then stop. Our life as a Christian is to be characterized by persistent prayer.

There is an implication in what Jesus says about persistence that sometimes baffles the one who is praying. The very fact that we have to be persistent tells us that the Father-King, who has promised to give us whatever we ask in Jesus' name, sometimes still does not give us what we ask right away. He encourages us to pray with confidence and then withholds from us the thing for which we pray. Reflecting on this fact, Andrew Murray states,

> O what a deep heavenly mystery this is of persevering prayer. The God who has promised, who longs, whose fixed purpose it is to give the blessing, holds it back. It is to Him a matter of such deep importance that His friends on earth should know and fully trust their rich Friend in heaven, that He trains them, in the school of answer delayed, to find out how their perseverance really does prevail, and what the mighty power is they can wield in heaven, if they do but set themselves to it.[37]

The temptation for us when the Father-King delays an answer is to stop praying. We perhaps think that God hasn't heard us or doesn't want to give us what we have asked for. There may be times when this is true. For example, after praying three times for his thorn in the flesh to be removed, the apostle Paul finally understood from the Lord that it was better for him that it not be removed (2 Corinthians 12:8,9). Then he stopped praying that prayer. Remember, however, that Paul received a definite answer from the Lord before he ceased praying. Unless we are sure of the Lord's answer to our prayers, Jesus encourages us to keep on praying. Again, Andrew Murray says,

> Of all the mysteries of the prayer world, the need of persevering prayer is one of the greatest. That the Lord, who is so loving and longing to bless, should have to be supplicated time after time, sometimes year after year, before the answer comes, we cannot easily understand. It is also one of the greatest practical difficulties in the exercise of believing prayer. When, after persevering supplication, our prayer remains unanswered, it is often easiest for our slothful flesh, and it has all the appearance of pious submission, to think that we must now cease praying, because God may have His secret reason for withholding His answer to our request.[38]

It is the "whatever" of Jesus that keeps us persistent in prayer. Persistence is simply holding on to this promise. God's promises are eternal and unfailing.

What then, should we ask from our Father-King with such boldness and persistence? In the next chapter we will take up our petitions to the Father-King.

10

Our Petitions to Our Father-King

In an ancient court, why would someone seek to have an audience with a king? Perhaps a man has broken the laws of the kingdom and asks to be allowed to beg for the king's mercy before his execution. Perhaps the citizens of the kingdom want to come before the king to praise him for the wonderful and fair way in which he has ruled them. Maybe the king has granted his subjects gifts, and they seek to come before him with thanks. There might be a poor peasant who seeks to bring a request to the king to provide charity for himself and his family so they don't starve. Or maybe there is a rich official who boldly asks the king to grant him an important position in the kingdom. Then there also might be the occasional citizen who asks to see the king on behalf of someone else. He might beg the king to show leniency to a man accused of a crime. Or perhaps he requests that the king show favor to a person who has demonstrated faithfulness and fairness in his business dealings. Any number of other situations could be listed that might be a reason for a person to request an audience with a king.

The Scriptures indicate that many similar situations may bring us before our heavenly Father-King. When our Father-King granted us an audience through Jesus Christ our Savior, he opened the door for all kinds of conversations to be carried on. Let's first consider the kinds of conversations that the people of the Bible carried on with their Father-King and then consider what kinds we carry on in our lives.

God's people gave praise and adoration

Oftentimes God's people simply talked to God about how great he is and the great things he had done and was doing for them. This kind of prayer we call *adoration,* or *praise.* For example, Nehemiah began his prayer to the Lord, "O LORD, God of heaven, the great and awesome God, who keeps his covenant of love with those who love and obey his commands, let your ear be attentive and your eyes open to hear the prayer your servant is praying before you day and night for your servants, the people of Israel" (Nehemiah 1:5,6). Another example would be the disciples' prayer after Peter and John had been released from prison: "When they heard this, they raised their voices together in prayer to God. 'Sovereign Lord,' they said, 'you made the heaven and the earth and the sea, and everything in them'" (Acts 4:24). It is great praise to list a person's good qualities or great accomplishments. This is especially true of God, who deserves to have us recognize his greatness and goodness. In Psalm 103 the psalmist lifts his voice to acclaim the Lord: "Praise the LORD, O my soul; all my inmost being, praise his holy name. Praise the LORD, O my soul, and forget not all his benefits" (verses 1,2). Then he continues by describing all of God's wonderful benefits.

God's people pleaded for mercy

There are also examples in the Scripture of believers pleading for mercy and forgiveness from the divine King. Moses did this for the people of Israel when they sinned against the Lord at Mount Sinai by making the golden calf (Exodus 32:11-13). Abraham repeatedly pleaded for mercy on behalf of Lot and his family when the Lord announced his impending destruction of Sodom and Gomorrah (Genesis 18:22-32). David sought the Lord's compassion after his terrible sins involving Bathsheba and her husband Uriah (Psalm 51). Daniel confessed the sins of Israel that had caused the exile of Israel to Babylon and pleaded with the Lord to forgive and show mercy to the remnant who were still alive (Daniel 9:4-19). Ezra and Nehemiah both prayed for forgiveness and mercy on the exiles who had returned to Jerusalem and yet had still broken the covenant laws (Ezra 9:6-15; Nehemiah 1:5-11). Many of the psalms are cries for mercy from distraught believers who are hoping for leniency and love from the Father-King (Psalms 6 and 130, for example). Even the thief's words from the cross, "Remember me when you come into your kingdom" (Luke 23:42), are a request for forgiveness and mercy.

God's people gave thanks

Another type of prayer we find in Scripture is the prayer of thanks. As could be expected, the book of

Psalms has many prayers of thanks. One that has become quite familiar to us is Psalm 136:1: "Give thanks to the LORD, for he is good. His love endures forever." Jesus teaches us to pray this kind of prayer in the account of the healing of the ten lepers. Little children in Sunday school learn about those ten men who were sick with leprosy. The lepers cried out to Jesus for healing. Jesus simply instructed them to show themselves to the priest, and while they were on their way, they were healed. Only one man, a Samaritan, returned to give thanks to Jesus for this blessing. Jesus asked, "Were not all ten cleansed? Where are the other nine?" (Luke 17:17). Giving thanks is an important kind of prayer for us to pray. It shows that we have truly appreciated all that our Father-King has done for us in answer to our prayers. Jesus himself gave thanks before he ate meals (Matthew 14:19; 15:36). Sunday after Sunday, in the words of institution to the Lord's Supper, we hear how Jesus took bread and wine and gave thanks. Paul likewise gave thanks for the food he was about to eat while on the ship headed for Rome that was shipwrecked on Malta shortly afterward (Acts 27:35).

God's people cried for help

Many believers spoke to the Lord in prayer when they needed help or aid. When Abraham's servant was trying to find a wife for Isaac, he turned to the Lord and asked for his help (Genesis 24). Gideon asked the Lord to make a fleece wet and then dry as assurance that the Lord was really going to be with him in his battle against Midian (Judges 6:36-40). Jonah cried out to the Lord for help when he was sinking into the sea (Jonah 2:2). In the New Testament, everyone who came to Jesus asking to be healed or cured was bringing this kind of prayer. The church in Jerusalem was praying for the Lord's aid for Peter when he was locked up in prison by Herod (Acts 12:5).

God's people pray for blessings for themselves and others

Scripture records that believers prayed for things both for themselves as well as for others. Manoah, the father of Samson, prayed that the Lord would teach him how to raise the special child he had promised to him (Judges 13:8). Samson prayed to the Lord for strength (16:28). Young King Solomon prayed that the Lord would give him discernment so that he could rule wisely (1 Kings 3:9). Zechariah, the father of John the Baptist, prayed for a son for himself and Elizabeth (Luke 1:13). The Lord Jesus teaches us to pray for ourselves in the Lord's Prayer when we pray, "Give us today our daily bread" (Matthew 6:11). Paul asked to have his thorn in the flesh taken away (2 Corinthians 12:7,8). Or we could simply quote the command of Jesus to "ask and it will be given to you" (Luke 11:9). It is not wrong to make requests for things for ourselves.

According to Scripture, it is just as proper to make requests for others. Isaac prayed about Rebekah's barrenness (Genesis 25:21). Moses prayed—sometimes at Pharaoh's request—that the plagues be removed from Egypt (Exodus 8–10). Jesus prayed for his disciples and all believers (John 17:6-26). Paul often encouraged his fellow Christians to pray for him and for his ministry (Romans 15:30-32; Ephesians 6:19,20). Paul also assured his fellow brothers and sisters in the faith that he was constantly praying to God for them (2 Thessalonians 1:11,12). Moreover, James explicitly commands us, "Pray for each other" (5:16).

Scripture even records Jesus' command to pray for our enemies. In his Sermon on the Mount, Jesus teaches, "Love your enemies and pray for those who persecute you, that you may be sons of your Father in heaven" (Matthew 5:44,45). Perhaps a comment on this passage might be in order. When Jesus says to pray for those who persecute us, what kind of prayer are we to pray for them? Are we to pray that God would cut them down and punish them? From the parallel passage in Luke's gospel, it is clear that this is not what we are to pray: "Bless those who curse you, pray for those who mistreat you" (6:28). Here Jesus expresses a parallel between blessing those who curse us and praying for those who abuse or mistreat us. The correspondence between "bless" and "pray" clearly indicates that our prayers for our abusers are ones of forgiveness and mercy. So also in Matthew, this is how we are "sons of [our] Father in heaven" (5:45). Just as our Father in heaven loves his enemies and shows them mercy, so also we are truly chips off the old block, if you will, when we likewise forgive and ask for mercy toward our enemies. Two outstanding examples of this are Jesus and Stephen. Jesus prayed, "Father, forgive them, for they do not know what they are doing" (Luke 23:34), as the soldiers hatefully drove nails through the hands of this "no-good drifter" from Galilee. Stephen also forgave those who were stoning him to death and prayed, "Lord, do not hold this sin against them" (Acts 7:60).

What about prayers for God's judgment against our enemies?

Considering what has just been said, how are we to view those psalms and other passages in Scripture that pray for God's judgment upon others? David, for example, often prayed that the Lord would punish his enemies. Just one example would be the words of Psalm 59:12,13: "For the sins of their mouths, for the words of their lips, let them be caught in their pride. For the curses and lies they utter, consume them in wrath, consume them till they are no more. Then it will be known to the ends of the earth that God rules over Jacob."

First, note that David is not praying such things upon those whom he simply dislikes. He is speaking to the Lord about those who are living in sin. The rest of the psalm describes these people as "bloodthirsty" and "fierce" men (verses 2,3). They commit violent acts and speak slander against God's people. They do this in defiance of the Lord's ability to punish them or protect his people. Ultimately, these are not David's enemies but enemies of the Lord himself, who had chosen David and the people of Israel as his own. To Abraham, years before this, the Lord had said that he would bless those who blessed him and curse those who cursed him and his descendants (Genesis 12:3).

Second, note that David's final hope in asking the Lord to bring judgment on these evildoers is that the Lord himself will be glorified (Psalm 59:13). These people had defied the Lord. By their actions and attitudes, they had blasphemed. The Lord's honor was being called into question. David wants the Lord to act not so that he can have vengeance on them but, rather, so that the Lord might vindicate himself and cause himself to be glorified among the nations.

Even when David says in the second half of Psalm 59:9, "God will go before me and will let me gloat over those who slander me," he is not as much thumbing his nose at his enemies as he is praising God, who is his strength and fortress—something he had just confessed at the beginning of this verse. That God would let him gloat over his enemies is not a vindictive desire on David's part, but evidence of the wonderful faithfulness of God to his promise: the Lord carries out justice for his oppressed.

When considering these prayers of judgment against enemies, we need also to keep in mind some other passages of Scripture. Our Lord wants us to harmonize our thoughts with his thoughts. Our Lord loves his enemies, but he also hates all who do wrong. Psalm 5:5 makes this very clear: "The arrogant cannot stand in your presence; you hate all who do wrong." We want to be like our Father in heaven by loving our enemies. But just as our Father in heaven hates those who continue to act wickedly and hates their wicked deeds, so we also hate evil with a godly hatred. "To fear the LORD is to hate evil" (Proverbs 8:13). Paul reminds us in Romans, "Love must be sincere. Hate what is evil; cling to what is good" (12:9). We understand with the writer of Ecclesiastes that there is "a time to love and a time to hate" (3:8). This means that just as our Father-King loves all people and wants them to be saved, so will we. This will prompt us to pray even for our enemies, with the hope that by God's mercy and grace they might repent and come to faith and be saved. At the same time, our Father-King hates evil and is abhorred by it. He promises to crush and judge all those who do evil and blaspheme his name. So also we will hate evil and pray that God shows himself to be holy among those who do evil and refuse to repent. We may also pray for God to demonstrate his true justice by bringing judgment on those who blaspheme him or recklessly and deliberately violate his commands. Notice that the emphasis is not on our being vindicated or a desire to see others suffer and gleefully savor their destruction. Rather, the desire is that God might be glorified over those who defy him and try to steal his glory for themselves.

Finally, Jesus praised the church of Ephesus, saying, "You have this in your favor: You hate the practices of the Nicolaitans, which I also hate" (Revelation 2:6). All hatred is not wrong—such as when we hate the things that God hates. David is actually justifying his prayers for judgment upon the wicked when he prays to the Lord, "Do I not hate those who hate you, O LORD, and abhor those who rise up against you? I have nothing but hatred for them; I count them my enemies" (Psalm 139:21,22). Not only is this a justification, but it is a necessity for those who claim to be God's children. We can do nothing less than what our Father in heaven does. Since he hates evil and falsehood, we must hate it also. We glorify him when we ask him to be what he is and act as he must according to his just nature. The one caution for us is to be sure that we first look inward and repent before we pray such a prayer so that we are not caught up in vengeance and not filled with a hatred that does not flow out of our love for God's holiness and glory.

For what things do we pray?

Now that we have looked at the various kinds of prayers that are apparent in the Scriptures, let us consider what kinds of prayers we are praying and compare the two. The following description of what we are praying is only a suggestion based on this author's survey, which asked a sampling of Christians to indicate the things for which they prayed. According to this survey, among the 1,287 persons who responded, 92 percent indicated that their prayers included thanksgiving to God. Eighty-four percent said that they confessed their sins in prayer. Seventy-eight percent said they prayed prayers asking for guidance in making decisions. Sixty-six percent asked for deliverance from some trouble. Seventy-five percent said they asked for great faith or some other spiritual blessing for themselves or for others. Sixty-eight percent asserted that they gave praise to God. Sixty-four percent have asked for physical things for others in prayer, while 58 percent have asked for physical things for themselves. Only 37 percent have prayed for the Holy Spirit, and 19 percent have complained about something to God in prayer.

Respondents to this survey were allowed to mark as many things as they prayed for. Then they were asked to select the two things that they felt they prayed for most often. In other words, of all the things that they might have prayed for, which things dominated their prayers? While not everyone responded to this question, 37 percent of those who did indicated that most often they give thanks to God in prayer. Second to giving thanks was confessing sins and asking for forgiveness, at 32 percent. Twenty-one percent said that most often they pray for guidance in making decisions. In a separate question, 77 percent answered yes when asked if they had ever prayed for their enemies.

Conclusions

What conclusions can we draw from the results of this survey? It appears that many of God's people today are praying many good prayers. It is good to see that thanksgiving is at the top of the list, both of things prayed for and of things prayed for most often. If we truly recognize who our Father-King is and what he has already done for us—especially at the cross through the sacrifice of his Son, Jesus Christ—then it seems that thanksgiving ought to top our list. We do indeed have much for which to be thankful. It is also good that we remember who we are before the Father-King. The fact that confession and asking for forgiveness is also high on the list—both of things prayed for and things prayed for most often—suggests that we do remember that our approach to the King is only through his grace and mercy. He promises to forgive those who come to him with humble and penitent hearts, and it appears that God's people are talking to him about their sins and asking for his mercy. This is to his glory and our blessing.

Another thing that is good to see is that God's people are not praying primarily for physical things. Prayers for spiritual blessings for ourselves and others were higher on the list than physical blessings. It is good for us to follow the promise of our Savior when he said to seek first the kingdom of heaven, trusting that all these things (food, clothes, and the like) will be given to us as well (Matthew 6:33). Requests for spiritual blessings ought to be given primary place in our prayers. The relationship between requests for physical things and spiritual things evident in the Lord's Prayer also teaches us that priority. Jesus gives us one petition for physical blessings ("Give us today our daily bread") and six regarding our spiritual welfare and the welfare of his kingdom. If we have learned to keep out of the rut of "gimme" prayers, that is good. If we are still struggling to get out of that rut, then we need to fill ourselves with God's Word so that our minds will be lifted out of the depths of self to the heights of the mind of God.

While praise was further down on the list than we might like to see it, considering all the encouragements to praise the Lord in Scripture, this might not be a clear indication of the amount of praise that God's people are doing. The survey may not have differentiated this category clearly enough. Many might have included praise in the response of giving thanks. In that case, it does rank as one of the most offered types of prayers.

The one place there might be quite a bit of room for improvement would be in requests for the Holy Spirit. Jesus specifically mentions praying for the Holy Spirit (Luke 11:13). He tells us that our Father in heaven is eager to give us the Holy Spirit. It would seem, then, that we ought to be praying for the Holy Spirit more regularly. From the survey it appears that nearly two-thirds of the respondents had never prayed for the Holy Spirit at all. This seems to be out of line with Jesus' desire for our prayers. Even if this percentage is off by quite a bit, it seems we could all learn to pray more earnestly for this special blessing, which our Father is eager to give.

This study has certainly not exhausted the list of things for which we might pray. It is only an attempt to help us realize the variety of conversations with our Father-King that may be listed under the general heading of prayer. Just as a subject of a kingdom may come to his or her sovereign and speak in a variety of ways, so we may come to our Father-King in just as many ways. Yet whenever we come to him and respond to his goodness and invitation to us to speak with him, we are praying. The question is, What will be his response after we have offered our prayers? This we will discuss in the next chapter.

11

The Father-King Answers Prayer

Ancient kings answer requests

Once again keeping the picture of an earthly king before us, we may gain some insight into the manner in which our Father-King answers our prayers. It is assumed in this chapter that we are primarily discussing prayers that make a request of the Father-King rather than prayers of praise and thanks, which really aren't looking for responses.

We might consider the scriptural account of Joseph and his brothers in Egypt (Genesis 42). Joseph was a ruler in Egypt. Pharaoh had given him authority over everything except Pharaoh himself. This was especially true of the storehouse of grain in Egypt. So when Joseph's brothers went down to Egypt, they appeared before Joseph rather than Pharaoh. They came to make a request for food so that they would not starve during the severe famine that had crippled Canaan as well. Yet Joseph did not immediately grant their request. In fact, knowing what Joseph did about his brothers, he knew that it was not in their best interest simply to give them grain. They needed to come to grips with their actions of years ago so that they could receive Joseph as their brother again. The point is that the king—Joseph, in this case—delayed an answer to a request, for the good of those who were making the request.

On the other hand, when we read the story of Nehemiah, we see a different response by his king (chapter 2). Nehemiah brought a request to Artaxerxes, king of Persia, that he might return to Jerusalem and help the people of his race rebuild their homeland and especially its capital, Jerusalem. Artaxerxes did not hesitate. He immediately commanded that Nehemiah return to his homeland and provided him with supplies for his journey and undertaking. Here we see an ancient king who did not delay but granted a request immediately.

The way ancient kings treated their subjects is similar to the way parents in families treat their children. Parents often receive requests from their children for various things. Yet parents have the wisdom to know that some things they can give their children right away, while other things must wait. Still other things their children may never have. If a five-year-old asks for help with a puzzle, most parents would help immediately. If a 12-year-old asks for a car, however, wise parents will tell their child that it will be a few more years before she will be ready for a car. They might give her a bicycle instead. Or they might simply tell her to wait. Another child might ask his parents for permission to see a movie rated NC-17, but his parents will deny his request and never consider granting it to him, for his own good.

The Father-King answers requests

If earthly kings and parents deal with their subjects and children in this way, it should not surprise us if our Father-King, in his vast wisdom, deals with his children in a similar fashion. Our Father-King may grant us our requests immediately. When Elijah prayed to the Lord at Mount Carmel and asked him to send fire to burn up the sacrifice on the altar and show that he was the true God, the Lord answered Elijah immediately (1 Kings 18:36-38). Abraham's servant, we are told, wasn't even finished praying when the Lord answered and sent Rebekah to him (Genesis 24:15).

The wise Father in heaven, however, did not always answer the requests of his children on earth in this immediate fashion. Undoubtedly, Abraham often pleaded with the Lord for the son he had been promised. For 25 years the Lord responded "not yet." Hannah prayed year after year for a son (1 Samuel 1:3-11). The Lord delayed giving her the son she so desired. A significant example of a delayed answer to a prayer is the account of Mary and Martha when their brother, Lazarus, was sick and died (John 11:1-44). These two faithful sisters, believing in the power of Jesus to heal, had sent a message to Jesus when Lazarus was only sick, asking Jesus to come and heal him. The gospel of John shows us that Jesus *deliberately* did not go immediately to the sisters and answer this prayer. From a human point of view, it appears to us that Jesus didn't care. The gospel, however, teaches us that Jesus had a higher good in mind for Mary and Martha. The higher good was that they might realize more fully who Jesus was. They believed that he had power over sickness. Yet they did not fully comprehend that Jesus was the very "resurrection and the life" (verse 25). Jesus had power over death itself. By not responding to their request immediately, Jesus had the opportunity to show them his true nature. They learned that he was Lord not only of life, but also of death. He delayed for their good. He taught them to trust and pray to him in any trouble—even if that trouble intensifies.

We can learn much about God's answers to our prayers from Mary and Martha's experience. So often our prayers fly to the Lord with great urgency because we see a "life-or-death" situation before us. We pray with great earnestness because we fear that time will run out on God's power and ability to help. When God delays and the situation worsens, we almost feel ourselves begin to give up on the Lord. Perhaps we stop praying because we feel the situation has slipped beyond God's reach and he will no longer be able to help. If only he had answered us sooner! How small our faith sometimes is! But the power of the Father-King has no limits. Even death itself is under his total control. Therefore, we need to pray with complete trust and confidence in his promises. He hears every prayer that is offered in Jesus' name. If God hears, then for Jesus' sake he also answers. Of this we can be absolutely sure. Reflect on these words of wisdom from the Reformer:

> As he [a Christian] undertakes to pray in compliance with God's command and in reliance on His promise, he offers it to God in the name of Christ, and he knows that what he asks for will not be denied him. And he actually experiences God's help in every need. Even if he is not immediately delivered from his distress, he knows nonetheless that his prayer is pleasing to God and is heard; and he knows

that God enables him to bear and overcome his distress. This ability is tantamount to the removal of the trouble.[39]

There are times when God doesn't give us what we ask for. This does not mean that he hasn't heard and answered our prayers. It does mean that he has chosen to answer them in accord with what his children always ask: "Not my will, but yours be done." In other words, he has determined that his will is the best for us and that it would be better to not give us what we have requested. Jesus' prayer in the Garden of Gethsemane is an outstanding example of this. The Lord could have granted Jesus' prayer and removed the cup of suffering from Jesus. This, however, would not have been the best thing according to God's will. The world would have lost its salvation. The Savior would not have reached his glory through suffering. In order for Jesus to accomplish God's will, his Father had to say no to his request in the garden. Jesus accepted this. He knew his Father would do what was best and left it in his hands.

The apostle Paul learned this same lesson. Paul prayed to the Lord that God might remove "a thorn in [his] flesh" (2 Corinthians 12:7). We don't know exactly what Paul's thorn was, but it is clear that Paul felt it was hindering his ministry. He felt that he could be a better apostle and reach more people if the Lord removed his thorn. He was so convinced of this that he pleaded with the Lord three times to take it away. When the Lord clearly said no, then Paul stopped praying. The Lord explained to Paul, "My grace is sufficient for you, for my power is made perfect in weakness" (verse 9). The Lord's will was accomplished by Paul's keeping the thorn. Paul learned to trust the Lord and not his own wisdom. If it was best for God's kingdom for Paul to keep his thorn, then he would gladly do so.

When we pray, we aren't always aware of what the Lord's answer is to our prayer. Paul had the advantage that the Lord gave an answer directly to him. We, on the other hand, don't always know what the answer is. As we noted earlier, we are to persist in asking until we do see an answer. If we do finally see that the Lord has said no to the specific thing we are requesting, then we can be assured that this is God's will for us and is best for us. Finally, then, such a "no" answer is not really no at all. For we have prayed for his will to be done—and so it has been.

It is also important for us to realize that God's purposes are not always easy for us to understand. He may grant one person what he does not grant to another. He may say yes to our prayer one time and no to the same request on another occasion. When this happens, it has nothing to do with whether we have prayed properly or not. It has everything to do with God's purposes and his divine wisdom.

An example of this is found in Acts chapter 12. As Luke tells the history of the early church, he describes to us the wicked ways of Herod Agrippa. Herod persecuted the members of the early church. He arrested some of them and put them in prison and executed them. James the brother of John, a disciple and apostle of Jesus, was arrested. He was then executed at Herod's command. Shortly after this, Peter was also arrested and imprisoned. Herod intended to put him to death too, after the Passover was completed. We are told that the church was "earnestly praying to God for him" (verse 5). The Lord answered that prayer. He sent his angel to release Peter so that Peter could continue to proclaim the name of Jesus.

Isn't it right for us to assume that the believers would also have been earnestly praying for James? Can we imagine that they cared nothing for James and only prayed for Peter? Of course not! They surely would have prayed for James in whatever time they had before Herod executed him. Yet the Lord did not rescue James. James too was an apostle. He too was proclaiming the gospel of Christ. Yet in his wisdom and according to his purpose, the Lord saw fit to allow James to die and Peter to remain to preach. The church prayed for both. These believers offered godly prayers. The Lord's response, however, was different according to his purpose. So also when we pray, we must be aware that the Lord's ways are beyond our understanding. Yet, whatever those ways are, they are for our good and for the good of his church. He always knows best.

There are times, however, when the Lord denies our prayers simply because they are not proper prayers. We noted in the section regarding confident prayer that doubt is a hindrance to our prayers. James wrote that those who pray with doubt in their hearts shouldn't expect to receive anything from the Lord (1:6,7). Peter tells husbands that their prayers will be hindered if they are living with their wives in such a way that they are mistreating them (1 Peter 3:7). Such activity would indicate a failure to live in true repentance. It would be evidence of unbelief.

Prayers prayed in unbelief are hindered before the Lord and will not be answered. For this reason, our prayers must always begin with what we spoke about earlier in this book—a cry (or at least an attitude that begs) for mercy on us. "To call on God and to say, 'Have mercy,' is not a great deal of work. But to add the particle 'on me'—this is really what the Gospel inculcates so earnestly, and yet we experience how hard it is for us to do it. This 'on me' hinders almost all our prayers, when it ought to be the only reason and highest occasion for praying."[40] When we forget to begin our prayers with "have mercy *on me*," we are likely forgetting that we are not worthy to ask for anything before the King because of our disobedience. If we approach without such humility, we are approaching in great presumption and self-righteousness. The gospel, however, tells us of a Savior who has erased the guilt of our disobedience and earned for us the right to pray. This good news compels us to come boldly, begging mercy for Jesus' sake. It empowers our prayers and assures us of an answer. When the gospel permeates our prayers, then we speak the words "have mercy on me" with wonder and delight. For the gospel assures us that the King has been merciful to us. He has granted us an audience and vowed to give us whatever we ask of him in his Son's name.

Does prayer change God?

Sometimes the question is asked, Does God ever change his course of action because of prayer?

There are Bible stories that seem to indicate that he does. For example, King Hezekiah once became ill, and the Lord told him through Isaiah that he was going to die from the illness. Then Hezekiah prayed, and the Lord announced that he would add 15 years to Hezekiah's life (2 Kings 20:1-6). God announced to Nineveh that it would be destroyed in 40 days. When the city repented, God "had compassion and did not bring upon them the destruction he had threatened" (Jonah 3:10).

Yet we know that God has everything planned out from eternity (Psalm 139:16). He does not make up things as he goes along in his governance of the universe. God is changeless; he does not change his mind from one day to the next (Numbers 23:19; James 1:17).

The best we can do to harmonize these passages is to conclude that God has built our prayers into his overall governance of all things. So from his perspective, everything is determined. But from our perspective, things can happen differently when we pray.

Certainly, God wants us to pray with the understanding that prayer is effective. It changes things. In his amazing wisdom and grace, the Father allows himself to be influenced by our prayers. James 5:16 says, "The prayer of a righteous man is powerful and effective." Jesus promised, "Ask and it will be given to you; seek and you will find; knock and the door will be opened to you" (Matthew 7:7). James goes so far as to say, "You do not have, because you do not ask God" (James 4:2).

Only the triune God can answer prayer

It is important, finally, that our prayers be directed only to the King. Prayers that are directed to anything or anyone else will not be answered. The prayers of the prophets of Baal at Mount Carmel were not answered because they were directed to idols and images, which had no power to answer them (1 Kings 18:26-29). So also will prayers directed to the virgin Mary or to saints or angels fail to be answered. These individuals have no power to grant our requests. Nor has the King given us any command to bring our prayers to them. For this reason, the Lutheran Church has always taught, as Scripture teaches, that our prayers must be directed only to the triune God.

Yet in a catalog from a publisher affiliated with the Roman Catholic Church, one can find a book entitled

Prayers to Mary. Indeed, in the *Catechism of the Catholic Church* it is stated,

> The Church rightly honors "the Blessed Virgin with special devotion. From the most ancient times the Blessed Virgin has been honored with the title of 'Mother of God,' to whose protection the faithful fly in all their dangers and needs...." The liturgical feasts dedicated to the Mother of God and Marian prayer, such as the rosary, an "epitome of the whole Gospel," express this devotion to the Virgin Mary.[41]

Even with the concession which is given that this "special devotion . . . differs essentially from the adoration which is given to the incarnate Word and equally to the Father and the Holy Spirit," the statement clearly says that prayers are to be offered and cries for help are to be made to the virgin Mary. There is no scriptural reference given showing that this is a command of the Lord. The fact is, there is nothing in Scripture that instructs God's people to pray to the virgin Mary or to cry to her for help. Still, the *Ave Maria* ("Hail Mary"), a common Roman Catholic prayer to Mary, states, "Pray for us sinners, now and at the hour of our death." The *Catechism of the Catholic Church* elaborates on this by saying, "By asking Mary to pray for us, we acknowledge ourselves to be poor sinners and we address ourselves to the 'Mother of Mercy.'"[42]

Along a similar line, the *Catechism of the Catholic Church* also instructs that prayers be made to the "saints."

> The witnesses who have preceded us into the kingdom, especially those whom the Church recognizes as saints, share in the living tradition of prayer by the example of their lives, the transmission of their writings, and their prayer today.... Their intercession is their most exalted

service to God's plan. We can and should ask them to intercede for us and for the whole world."[43]

In contrast to this, the foundational doctrinal statement of the Lutheran Church, the Augsburg Confession, states,

> The Scriptures do not teach us to pray to the saints or seek their help, for the only mediator, propitiation, highpriest, and intercessor whom the Scriptures set before us is Christ. He is to be prayed to, and he has promised to hear our prayers. Such worship Christ especially approves, namely, that in all afflictions he be called upon. "If anyone sins, we have an advocate with the Father," etc. (I John 2:1).[44]

Not only isn't prayer to Mary or the saints commanded anywhere in Scripture, but because it is not commanded or even mentioned, there can be no certainty of prayers that are prayed to them or to the intercession that they are supposed to offer for us. The Apology of the Augsburg Confession states, "Our Confession affirms only this much, that Scripture does not teach us to invoke the saints or to ask their help. Neither a command nor a promise nor an example can be shown from Scripture for the invocation of the saints; from this it follows that consciences cannot be sure about such invocation."[45]

Furthermore, since we do have a command of the Lord to pray to Jesus Christ, and since he is specifically called our mediator and intercessor, it is a dishonor to Christ to credit the saints with the work and office that rightfully belongs only to Jesus. Jesus alone is our propitiator, that is, the one who goes between us and God and makes peace.

> There must be a Word of God to assure us that God is willing to have mercy and to answer those who call upon him through this propitiator. For Christ there is such a

promise (John 16:23), "If you ask anything of the Father, he will give it to you in my name." But for the saints there is no such promise, and hence consciences cannot be sure that we shall be heard if we invoke the saints.[46]

The same thoughts apply also to the popular practice of praying to angels. We treasure the angels as powerful helpers sent from God, but the Bible does not encourage us to pray to angels. They are created beings, and to give them the honor and worship due to the Lord is idolatry. When the apostle John was tempted to worship an angel, the angel stopped him (Revelation 19:10; 22:8,9).

To pray to Mary or the saints or angels, therefore, for the things we are assured of receiving through Christ is to place doubt into our prayers. Furthermore, it denies the very command of our King that instructs us to pray "in the name of Jesus." It is the merit of Jesus Christ and the favor that he has gained for us with the Father-King that gives us the guarantee of an answer to our prayers.

12

Handbook on Prayer

The purpose of a handbook

We have searched the Scriptures to learn what prayer is and how it is that we have the privilege of coming to the Lord in prayer. We have considered what Scripture teaches us about where and when to pray, as well as for what and for whom we ought to pray. We have learned the important attitude of our hearts that is necessary for prayer and the ways in which our King might answer our prayers. Above all, we have learned the importance of our Savior Jesus Christ, and his Holy Word in all of our praying. Yet perhaps we still feel a bit hesitant to pray. What if I say the wrong thing? To whom should I address my prayers? How do I keep from praying for inappropriate things? What are the proper words?

The answer to our fears would be a handbook on prayer. When someone gets a new job with a company, the new employee often receives a handbook that gives guidance. If employees follow the handbook, they are sure to do what they are supposed to do and to avoid what might not fit the company's policies. So also a handbook on prayer would give us guidance so that we are headed in the right direction in our prayer lives. It wouldn't give us all the prayers we will ever pray, but it would give us a guide—a pattern, if you will—to help us see what God-pleasing prayer is like. It would help us keep in line with what our Father-King wants us to pray and help us avoid some of the pitfalls of prayer that we need to avoid.

Such a handbook has been given to us. It is the prayer that Jesus taught to his disciples when they asked him, "Teach us to pray" (Luke 11:1). We call it the "Lord's Prayer," or sometimes it is called the "Our Father." While it is beyond the scope of this book to do an in-depth study of this model prayer from our Savior, we can at least look briefly at this prayer and gain some insights into how we might improve our prayer life by emulating this prayer in other prayers that we pray from our hearts. Before we look at this prayer, let us consider one small matter that will also lead us into the prayer that Jesus taught.

Father, Son, or Holy Spirit—to whom do I pray?

On more than one occasion, Christians have asked this author, "To whom should I pray?" With that question they were not asking me whether they should pray to some idol or god other than the triune God. Rather, they were asking, To which person of the triune God should we direct our prayers: Father, Son, or Holy Spirit? For this reason, when this author sent out his survey on prayer, he included a question concerning to whom the survey respondents directed their prayers. The question was worded in such a way that respondents could mark any of the answers that applied. The responses indicated that 83 percent of the 1,287 who completed the survey have addressed their prayers to "God." Fifty-seven percent have addressed them to the Father, 39 percent to the Son, and 37 percent to the Holy Spirit. In addition, 69 percent indicated that they prayed to Jesus. What is proper? To which person of the Trinity should we pray? By what title should we address our God?

We turn to Scripture for some insight. There is no doubt that we should address our prayers to the Father. Jesus said, "When you pray, go into your room, close the door and pray to your Father, who is unseen" (Matthew 6:6). Though the triune God is Father, Son, and Holy Spirit, Jesus specifically names the Father as the object of our prayers. Yet to make a rule and say that we therefore ought to only address our prayers to the Father would not be in keeping with the rest of Scripture.

Jesus also told his disciples, "Believe me when I say that I am in the Father and the Father is in me. . . . And I will do whatever you ask in my name, so that the Son may bring glory to the Father. You may ask me for anything in my name, and I will do it" (John 14:11,13,14). Jesus instructs his disciples to make requests of him so that he might answer their requests and bring glory to the Father. When Stephen prayed as he was being stoned to death, he addressed his prayer to "Lord Jesus" (Acts 7:59). Of particular note in the passage from John is Jesus' reference to the mystery of the Trinity: "I am in the Father and the

Father is in me." We cannot comprehend the amazing truth that Jesus and the Father are one. Yet it is on the basis of this divine truth that Jesus can say "pray to the Father" and at the same time say "pray to me" and this command is not contradictory in the least. This is the incomprehensible mystery of the Trinity that Scripture reveals to us.

Following this pattern, we can also comment on addressing prayers to the Holy Spirit. It is clear that we are to pray *for* the Holy Spirit (Luke 11:13). But no passage in Scripture teaches us to pray *to* the Holy Spirit by name. Yet considering the mystery of the Trinity, such a prayer would certainly be appropriate. Just as Isaiah witnessed the angels in heaven calling to one another, "Holy, holy, holy is the LORD Almighty" (6:3), so also whenever believers lift up their voices in praise to the Lord Almighty, this is a prayer to the Holy Spirit as well as to the Father and the Son. It is for this reason that the historic Christian church did not shy away from prayers addressed to the Holy Spirit. During the Pentecost season we may hear the words "Come, Holy Spirit, renew our hearts and kindle in us the fire of your love" spoken or sung in our churches.[47] These words come from the historic Christian liturgy. They clearly address the Holy Spirit with a prayer to increase our faith and our life of love—which, according to Scripture, is primarily the work of the Holy Spirit. Page through a Lutheran hymnal, and in the Pentecost section you will find any number of prayer-hymns that address the Holy Spirit.

To whom, then, should we address our prayers? The Scriptures would not prohibit us from addressing them to God, to the Father, to the Son, or to the Holy Spirit. Yet perhaps a passage from the pen of the apostle Paul can shed some light on the inner relationship of the persons of the triune God. Paul wrote, "Through him [Jesus] we both have access to the Father by one Spirit" (Ephesians 2:18). Notice that this passage is a clear reference to the triune God. It also reveals to us something about our prayers. "Access to the Father" tells us that the object of our prayers is the Father. "Through him [Jesus]" tells us that Jesus has gained for us the right to enter the Father's presence and bring a request to him. "By one Spirit" reminds us that prayer is a fruit of faith, which is the direct working of the Holy Spirit in our hearts. As we address our prayers to God, perhaps it is best for us to keep this relationship in mind.

The Lord's Prayer

This now brings us to the model prayer that Jesus gave to his disciples. While it is not the only way to pray, it is to be a pattern for us to follow. We take careful note, then, that Jesus teaches us to address our prayers to the "Father."

The prayer itself is given in two forms in the gospels. Luke's version, given in response to the request of Jesus' disciples to teach them how to pray, is as follows:

> Father,
> hallowed be your name,
> your kingdom come.
> Give us each day our daily bread.
> Forgive us our sins,
> > for we also forgive everyone who sins against us.
> And lead us not into temptation. (11:2-4)

Matthew's version, which is longer, was spoken by Jesus as an example of how not to pray like the pagans, who babble on with many words. Instead, Jesus offers this prayer as the proper way to pray:

> Our Father in heaven,
> hallowed be your name,
> your kingdom come,
> your will be done
>   on earth as it is in heaven.
> Give us today our daily bread.
> Forgive us our debts,
>   as we also have forgiven our debtors.
> And lead us not into temptation,
> but deliver us from the evil one. (6:9-13)

A pattern for prayer

As was mentioned earlier, this is a model prayer. This means that it is a pattern for us to follow, but it is not the only way for us to pray. Perhaps an illustration can help us to understand the importance of a pattern. Many people who sew use a pattern. When they follow the pattern, the company that produces that pattern is really guaranteeing to them that they will end up with an article of clothing like the one pictured on the cover. Yet many people who begin using such patterns gradually develop the ability to sew without a purchased pattern. Having learned basic concepts about sewing clothes from a pattern, they are able to apply their skills freely to other clothing they sew. But in the end, it is all still clothing.

So it is with our prayers. Jesus gives us a pattern in the Lord's Prayer. Especially as we are beginning to learn to pray, it is wise for us to use this pattern. By using it, we have the guarantee of our Savior that it will be heard and answered, for he himself has given us the proper words to say. Since it is given by the Son who knows his Father's will perfectly, there is no doubt that everything that is requested is perfectly in line with the Father's will and therefore will be granted. For this reason, there is no greater prayer we can pray. It is also for this reason that even when we have become familiar with how to pray, we will not want to set this prayer aside and never use it again. It is still the grandest of all prayers.

Yet just as people who sew venture out on their own to sew new clothes based on the pattern, so also Christians, as they gain confidence in their ability to pray, will also be able to pray other prayers that are not necessarily confined to the wording of the Lord's Prayer and yet are patterned according to it. It is for this value also that the Lord's Prayer needs to be diligently studied by us. Finally, when we can think of nothing else to pray, we can always go back to the pattern. In times of anguish or great joy, when no other words seem to come, we have a prayer that is certain to please and to bring great results: our Lord's Prayer.

Luther once said, "The Lord's Prayer is the greatest martyr on earth (as are the name and word of God). Everybody tortures and abuses it; few take comfort and joy in its proper use."[48] By this Luther meant that we all would do well to study the Lord's Prayer and mine its treasure so that when we pray it, we do not simply recite the words mechanically. Frequency of use, as when we speak it at every worship service and to close every meeting, can easily lead to empty repetition. To fight against this, we need to meditate carefully on the words that Jesus taught us to say, so that our spirits might be led to soar with them to the very throne of heaven in heartfelt pleas to the Father-King.

A child's prayer

Jesus teaches us first to whom we are praying and what our relationship is. It is simple and yet profound. We pray to "Our Father in heaven." It is not "my Father," but "*our* Father"—to remind us that we are part of the church, the communion of saints. As a collective whole, we pray to our Father in heaven. He is our Father because we are his children through faith in Jesus Christ. This address at once teaches us of the endearing relationship we have with him who is both our King and *Father*. As a Father who delights to listen to his child and grant his child's requests, so we are to approach the Lord of heaven and earth. There is love between us, thanks to Jesus.

Uphold the family name

The first petition, or request, is that we honor our Father's name. We do this when we keep his name holy, sacred, set apart. This doesn't just mean, as the Second Commandment states, that we refrain from vulgar and senseless uses of the Father's name. The Father's name is his reputation; that is, it is everything we know about him. In John 17:6, Jesus says, "I have revealed *you* to those whom you gave me out of the world." There the Greek literally says, "I have revealed your *name*." The Greek means what the English says. In Scripture a person's name means everything about him. Jesus didn't just reveal a name by which to call the Father. He revealed the Father's will and what he had done and is still doing to save us.

So for us to keep our Father's name holy means to protect and honor his will and his plan of salvation. In particular, that means to protect and honor God's Word and live according to it. In other words, God's name is kept holy when his Word is preached and taught truthfully and without error. If children lie or say things that their parents haven't said, the children bring dishonor to their family name. In the same way, to lie or misrepresent God's Word is to dishonor God. Similarly, if children are disobedient and constantly misbehaving, it also reflects on the family to which they belong. So too if we disobey the Lord and live contrary to his will, he is dishonored in the eyes of the world. The opposite is also true. Lives that conform to his holy will cause great glory to be given to the Father in heaven.

Rule us, King of righteousness

The second petition, or request, is that the Father's kingdom come. It is not an earthly, political kingdom for which we pray. Scripture tells us that Christ's kingdom is within us (Luke 17:21). It is the rule of Christ in our hearts by faith. This is also the Father's kingdom. He is the King of righteousness. Through faith in Jesus Christ as our Savior, the King credits to us the righteousness of his Son. This is the work of the Holy Spirit, who brings us to faith in Jesus so that we have this righteousness by faith. This work the Holy Spirit accomplishes through the preaching of the Word, for faith comes from hearing the message (Romans 10:17).

It is clear, then, that we are praying for the preaching and teaching of the Word when we pray this petition. When the Word, especially the gospel message, is proclaimed, then people are brought to faith. Through faith, God's rule is established and sustained and his kingdom comes. We pray both for ourselves and for mission work to those throughout the world who yet need to hear the gospel. In this way, the kingdom marches to the ends of the earth.

The Father's agenda is best

The third petition, or request, is for the Father's will to be done on earth as in heaven. In other words, as children of our heavenly Father, we want to follow his agenda. His agenda has already been established, namely, that his name be kept holy and his kingdom come. This divine agenda is carried out in and through his church. It may be that it requires suffering and crosses on the part of his children. Yet our Father's agenda is always best. It is also absolute. There is no alternative.

When we pray this petition, we are asking for two things. First, we are praying that through his Word the Holy Spirit would continue to lead us to accept our Father's agenda in our hearts. Our sinful nature constantly wants to establish its own agenda, with its own priorities. This petition is a prayer to defeat the influence of our sinful nature and to establish the rule of the Spirit in our hearts. Then we will both know our Father's agenda and consider it best.

Second, we are praying that the Lord would stop those things outside of us that also hinder the Lord's agenda from being accomplished. This would include the forces of Satan, as well as the influences of those who follow Satan in their lives. It would include the temptations of the things of this world. We do not have the power ourselves to overcome these things. In this petition we are praying for strength to resist evil, as well as for the Father's intervention to crush the forces of evil, which oppose the proclamation of the Word and the establishment of his kingdom.

"Things" are secondary, not sinful

The fourth petition, or request, is for "daily bread." Sandwiched between the first three and last three petitions, it is the only petition that specifically asks for earthly necessities for our physical bodies. In this one short petition is made our request for all the material things we need.

By the very fact that there is only one such petition, Jesus gives us an important pattern for our prayers. Though it is not wrong or improper to pray for the material things we need in life, they are to be secondary. We are to concern ourselves first with prayers for the kingdom of God and only secondarily for physical things. Indeed, Jesus tells us, "Seek first his kingdom and his righteousness, and all these things will be given to you as well" (Matthew 6:33). He says, "Your heavenly Father knows that you need them" (verse 32). Praying for these things keeps us mindful of the one who gives these things, so that we might always remember to receive them with thanks.

Quiet my conscience, contain my conceit

The fifth petition, or request, is that our Father would forgive us our sins as we have forgiven those who sin against us. By teaching us to pray this petition, Jesus is teaching us that we are sinners who have a need for forgiveness. Indeed, our sins are so many and so great that we have need to pray this petition every day. It is a plea that the Father in heaven would help us to recognize and trust in his forgiveness so that our consciences might be quieted and no longer trouble us. How wonderfully our Savior leads us to his cross in this prayer! He teaches us that all our prayers need to begin at the cross. There alone do we find forgiveness. There alone is the barrier between us and our God removed.

In the first three petitions, we pray for the Lord's kingdom and his glory; the fourth, for our physical well-being. As Jesus begins the last three petitions, which have to do with our spiritual well-being, he begins with the most important thing of all—forgiveness of our sins. This is at the heart of our faith. It is the pinnacle of our requests.

For without the forgiveness of sins, all is lost. Therefore, we pray, "Forgive us our sins," and what we ask in the Lord's Prayer, we indeed receive. This is the great blessing of this prayer and its petitions taught by the Savior himself. Our sins are indeed forgiven.

Yet this petition contains a warning from our Savior, because of our sinful nature, which so easily perverts God's grace. There is no forgiveness for the unrepentant and proud heart. It is the broken and contrite heart that our Father will not despise (Psalm 51:17). It is the humble whom he lifts up with forgiving love, while the proud he brings low and destroys. So if our hearts become conceited and refuse forgiveness to others after the Lord has freely forgiven our sins, then like the unmerciful servant, we will be cast into outer darkness (Matthew 18:23-35). Then there will be no forgiveness, for there is no true repentance. Jesus amplifies this petition in his commentary that follows the Lord's Prayer in Matthew's gospel: "If you forgive men when they sin against you, your heavenly Father will also forgive you. But if you do not forgive men their sins, your Father will not forgive your sins" (6:14,15). Our refusal to forgive others is a sign of a hard heart. It jeopardizes our own forgiveness because it is a sign of unbelief. We are praying in this petition that the Lord would keep us from such unbelief and conceit. Moreover, when we do forgive others, this petition is an assurance that our Lord has forgiven us. For a forgiving heart is the response of faith to the forgiveness that the Father has first granted us in Christ. "We love because he first loved us" (1 John 4:19).

Reinforcement, not relocation

The sixth petition, or request, is that our Father would not lead us into temptation. It is clear from Scripture that we are not to understand by this petition that our Father would ever tempt us to sin (James 1:13). Rather, we are surrounded on every side by temptations every day. These temptations come from outside through the devil and the evil society in which we live, which we often simply refer to as "the world." They also come from within us—that is, from our sinful nature. As long as we are on earth, temptations will assail us, for we cannot escape our own bodies, avoid the world, or hide from Satan. We are not praying in this petition for relocation or removal from all temptation.

In his High Priestly Prayer, recorded in John chapter 17, Jesus prays something similar to what he teaches us to pray in this petition. There, as he prayed for his disciples and knew that they were going to face some severe trials in the days ahead of them, he did not pray that the Father remove them from the world and spare them these trials. Rather, he prayed that the Father would sustain them and be with them so that they would not succumb to these temptations but would stand firm in the faith. So also Jesus is not teaching us to pray that we face no trials or temptations, but to pray that the Father would send his Holy Spirit to keep our faith strong through his Word so that we may resist temptations and struggle for the faith against every attack. It is a prayer for reinforcement, not relocation.

Destroy the devil's deeds

The final petition, or request, is that the Lord would deliver us from evil. The NIV uses the alternative wording of "the evil one"—namely, Satan, or the devil. This reminds us above all that as God's children, we are not just in a battle against evil. We are in mortal combat against the devil himself—the evil one.

Just as we could not overcome Satan to free ourselves from the eternal punishment of hell, so we cannot be victorious over him in our daily struggle to do the will of our heavenly Father. Jesus came to destroy the devil's work (1 John 3:8). In its context this passage refers primarily to the fact that Jesus has freed us from the rut of sinning. This is the result of his victory on the cross as well. Not only has Jesus delivered us from damnation, but he has also freed us from sin's dominion in our daily lives. We are no longer addicted to the devil's deeds, but as Christians recovering from that addiction, we are doing the will of our Father in heaven. Yet because we still bear the flesh of corruption, our daily lives will constantly be a struggle to do his will. Therefore, we pray for help. We pray that the Lord will daily destroy the devil's deeds in us so that we do not fall into sin. We pray that the Lord would help us to overcome, to run the race and finish, to fight the good fight of faith and lay hold of eternal life.

This is the final spiritual blessing that we ask for. It is the ultimate goal of all that we have prayed in the Lord's Prayer. Ultimately, we are praying the Lord's Prayer so that we might someday move from the kingdom of God in battle to the kingdom of God at rest in heaven.

Concluding words of praise

The reader may have noticed that when we quoted the two versions of the Lord's Prayer that are given in the gospels of Matthew and Luke, neither concluded with the familiar words, "For the kingdom, the power, and the glory are yours now and forever. Amen." This is because these words were not part of the Lord's Prayer as Jesus gave it. Early Christians added these words as they prayed the Lord's Prayer in church. They are certainly in harmony with other doxologies (words of praise) that we find in Scripture (1 Chronicles 29:11) and therefore are a fitting way for us to conclude our Lord's Prayer. They serve as a reminder to us that our *Father* in heaven, who lovingly invites our prayers, is also able to do what we ask. He is the all-powerful King with whom nothing is impossible. He alone deserves and receives all the glory!

Endnotes

[1] Andrew Murray, *With Christ in the School of Prayer* (Old Tappan, NJ: Fleming H. Revell Co., 1981), pp. 147,148.

[2] Murray, pp. 9,10.

[3] See exegetical brief "Is Abba 'Daddy'?" by John F. Brug in *Wisconsin Lutheran Quarterly*, Vol. 93, No. 4 (Fall 1996), p. 287.

[4] Martin Luther, *Luther's Works*, edited by Jaroslav Pelikan and Helmut T. Lehmann, American Edition (St. Louis: Concordia Publishing House; Philadelphia: Fortress Press, 1955–1986), Vol. 42, p. 87.

[5] Murray, pp. 122,123.

[6] Martin E. Lehmann, *Luther and Prayer* (Milwaukee: Northwestern Publishing House, 1985), pp. 11,12. (Luther quote from *Luther's Works*, Vol. 12, p. 312.)

[7] Oscar E. Feucht, *The Practice of Prayer* (St. Louis: Concordia Publishing House, 1956), pp. 22,23.

[8] Murray, pp. 123,124.

[9] Lehmann, p. 146. (Luther quote from *Luther's Works*, Vol. 51, p. 333.)

[10] Quoted in Feucht, p. 7.

[11] *The Lutheran Hymnal* (St. Louis: Concordia Publishing House, 1941) 454:2.
[12] Saint Augustine, *Commentary on the Lord's Sermon on the Mount with Seventeen Related Sermons*, The Fathers of the Church (New York: Fathers of the Church, Inc., 1951), Vol. 11, p. 240.
[13] *Luther's Works*, Vol. 24, p. 89.
[14] Lehmann, pp. 107,108. (Luther quote from *Luther's Works*, Vol. 42, p. 73.)
[15] Lehmann, pp. 69,70.
[16] *Luther's Works*, Vol. 42, p. 60.
[17] Lehmann, p. 129. (Luther quote from *Luther's Works*, Vol. 24, p. 87.)
[18] Lehmann, p. 111.
[19] *Together Forever* (Appleton, WI: Aid Association for Lutherans, 1997), p. 34.
[20] Gerhard Kittel, editor, *Theological Dictionary of the New Testament* (Grand Rapids: Wm. B. Eerdmans Publishing Co., 1964), Vol. II, p.790, footnote #181.
[21] Augustine, *Commentary on the Lord's Sermon on the Mount*, The Fathers of the Church, Vol. 11, p. 125.
[22] Tertullian, *Disciplinary, Moral and Ascetical Works*, The Fathers of the Church, Vol. 40, p. 182.
[23] Kittel, p. 790.
[24] Tertullian, *Disciplinary, Moral and Ascetical Works*, The Fathers of the Church, Vol. 40, p. 170.
[25] Clement of Rome, *The Apostolic Fathers*, The Fathers of the Church, Vol. 1, p. 32.
[26] Clement of Rome, *The Apostolic Fathers*, The Fathers of the Church, Vol. 1, p. 46.
[27] Lehmann, pp. 92,93.
[28] Feucht, pp. 25,26.
[29] Jill Briscoe, *Hush! Hush! It's time to pray—but how?* (Grand Rapids: Zondervan Publishing Corporation, 1978), p. 72.
[30] Parsons Technology, *Bible Illustrator*, "Prayer/Answer Promised/Rich and Generous," #2819, 6/1986.7.

[31] *Christian Worship: A Lutheran Hymnal* (Milwaukee: Northwestern Publishing House, 1993) 409:2.
[32] Parsons Technology, *Bible Illustrator*, "Prayer/Answer Promised/Hot Water Bottle and Doll," #2819, 6/1986.5.
[33] Briscoe, pp. 53,54.
[34] *Luther's Works*, Vol. 25, p. 460.
[35] Murray, p. 134.
[36] *Luther's Works*, Vol. 14, pp. 60,61.
[37] Murray, p. 49.
[38] Murray, p. 87.
[39] *Luther's Works*, Vol. 24, p. 241.
[40] *Luther's Works*, Vol. 12, p. 317.
[41] *Catechism of the Catholic Church* (Washington D.C.: United States Catholic Conference, Inc., Libreria Editrice Vaticana, 1994), par. 971, p. 253.
[42] *Catechism of the Catholic Church*, par. 2677, p. 644.
[43] *Catechism of the Catholic Church*, par. 2683, p. 645.
[44] Augsburg Confession, Article XXI:2-4, *The Book of Concord: The Confessions of the Evangelical Lutheran Church*, translated and edited by Theodore G. Tappert (Philadelphia: Fortress Press, 1959), p. 47.
[45] Apology of the Augsburg Confession, Article XXI:10, Tappert, p. 230.
[46] Apology of the Augsburg Confession, Article XXI:17, Tappert, p. 231.
[47] *Christian Worship*, p. 87.
[48] *Luther's Works*, Vol. 43, p. 200.

For Further Reading

Acker, J. W. *Teach Us to Pray*. St. Louis: Concordia Publishing House, 1961.

Brokering, Herbert F. *Luther's Prayers*. Minneapolis: Augsburg Publishing House, 1967.

Clement, Arthur J. *Pray, Christian, Pray!* Milwaukee: Northwestern Publishing House, 1993.

Feucht, Oscar E. *The Practice of Prayer*. St. Louis: Concordia Publishing House, 1956.

Lehmann, Martin E. *Luther and Prayer*. Milwaukee: Northwestern Publishing House, 1985.

Luther, Martin. Large Catechism, Part III: The Lord's Prayer. *The Book of Concord: The Confessions of the Evangelical Lutheran Church,* translated and edited by Theodore G. Tappert. Philadelphia: Fortress Press, 1959.

Scripture Index

Genesis
   3:15—15
   6,7—14
   12:3—131
   18:22-32—119,127
   19—14
   20:17,18—61
   24—128
   24:15—139
   25:21—129
   32:24-30—119
   32:26—119
   42—137

Exodus
   7–12—15
   8–10—129
   9:29,33—89
   14:21,22—13
   16—15
   32:11-13—127
   32:31,32—58
   34:6,7—15

Numbers
   23:19—145

Deuteronomy
   9:26—61

Joshua
   3:15-17—13
   6:20—13

Judges
   6:36,37—58
   6:36-40—128
   13:8—129
   16:28—129
   21:2—87

1 Samuel
    1:3-11—139
    1:9-16—98
    1:10—61
    1:11—57
    1:26—85
    12:19—58
    12:23—58

2 Samuel
    7:18—87

1 Kings
    1:15,16,22,23—18
    1:16—42
    3:9—129
    8—62
    8:54—83,89
    18:26-29—145
    18:36-38—139
    19:4—87

2 Kings
    4:33—62
    20:1-6—144
    20:2,3—62
    25—15

1 Chronicles
    29:11—163

2 Chronicles
    7:13-16—33
    20:6—12
    33:12,13—62

Ezra
    9:6,7—57
    9:6-15—127

Nehemiah
    1:4-11—62
    1:5,6—126
    1:5-7—57
    1:5-11—127
    1:11—18
    2—138
    9:2—85

Esther
    4:11,16—18
    5:2,3—42

Psalms
    5:5—132
    6—127
    6:6—88
    6:9—59
    14—19
    14:1,3—19
    32:3-6—56
    32:6—65
    47:6,7—12
    50:15—43
    51—45,127
    51:1-4,7—57
    51:17—160
    59:2,3—131
    59:9—131
    59:12,13—131
    59:13—131
    63:6—88
    66:17,18—21

95:3—12
96:2—55
98:1,4—55
103:1,2—55,127
130—127
136:1—55,128
139:2,4—99
139:16—144
139:21,22—133
141:2—89
145:18—65

Proverbs
1:20-33—22
8:13—132
15:29—16
20:2—20
28:9—23

Ecclesiastes
3:8—132

Isaiah
1:15-18—24
6:3—152
53:5—31
59:2—21

Jeremiah
10:10—14

Daniel
2:23—55
6:10—83,99
7:13,14—28
9:4-19—127

Jonah
1:17—14
2:2—128
2:2-9—62
2:10—14
3:10—15,144

Micah
3:1-4—25

Zechariah
7:13—25

Matthew
3:17—29
5:44—75
5:44,45—130
5:45—130
6:6—102,151
6:7—96
6:9—97
6:9-13—154
6:11—129
6:14,15—160
6:32—159
6:33—135,159
7:7—145
8:26—14
9:24,25—14
12:25—99
14:19—56,99,103,128
14:19-21—14
14:23—99
14:28-31—119
15:26—119
15:36—128
17:5—29

18:23-35—160
19:13—76
19:26—112
21:22—108
24:20—70
26:39—83
26:39-44—99
27:46—103
27:50,51—35

Mark
1:35—99
6:22-25—108
11:24—108
11:25—85
14:35—83
14:35,36—109
14:38—49

Luke
1:13—129
1:33—8
1:37—112
5:16—99,102
6:12—99
6:28—75,130
9:28—99
11:1—150
11:2-4—153
11:5-10—121
11:9—129
11:13—69,136,152
12:32—9
17:17—128
17:21—8,157
18:1-8—120
18:9-14—89

22:32—73
22:41—83
22:42—50
22:46—70
23:34—58,75,99,103,130
23:42—127

John
1:1—44
1:14—44
3:5—8
3:36—31
4:24—78
8:29—29
11:1-44—139
11:25—140
11:41—90
11:41,42—30,99,103
14:6—65
14:11,13,14—151
14:12-14—117
14:24—44
14:25,26—44
16:23—148
16:23,24—115
17—73,161
17:1—90,91
17:6—156
17:6-26—129
17:17—65
18:33,36—8

Acts
4:24—126
7:59—151
7:60—130
8:22—71

12:5—62,129,142
16:25—103
21:5—84,103
26:29—72
27:35—128

Romans
1:18—19
3—19
3:23—20,21
3:23-26—31
5:1,2—34
5:9,10—32
6:23—20
8:15—38
8:26—77,78,110
10:17—157
12:1—54
12:9—132
12:12—100
15:30,31—72
15:30-32—129
16:17—101

2 Corinthians
5:18,19—32
12:7—141
12:7,8—129
12:8,9—123
12:9—141

Galatians
4:6—78

Ephesians
2:3—20,30
2:18—34,153

3:12—34
3:14-20—84
3:20—112
6:18—79
6:19,20—129

Philippians
4:6—63,71

Colossians
1:3—56
4:12—63

1 Thessalonians
5:16-18—65
5:17—100

2 Thessalonians
1:11,12—129

1 Timothy
2:1,2—72
2:8—89
6:15,16—13

Titus
2:11,12—49
3:10—101

Hebrews
1:1,2—43
4:14-16—118
5:7—29
9:27—76
10:19-22—66
10:19-23—36
11:6—67

James
- 1:5-7—118
- 1:6,7—143
- 1:13—161
- 1:17—145
- 4:2—145
- 4:3—25
- 5:13—71
- 5:14—73
- 5:16—73,129,145
- 5:17,18—60

1 Peter
- 3:7—143
- 3:12—29,36

1 John
- 2:1—147
- 3:1—38
- 3:8—162
- 4:19—160
- 5:14,15—109

Jude
- 20—79

Revelation
- 2:6—133
- 19:10—148
- 22:8,9—148

Subject Index

Abba defined 38
adiaphoron, posture of prayer as 93
adoration and praise in prayer 126,127
anger of God 14-16,19,20,25, 27,30-32
answer to prayer 108-111,137-148
  delayed 122,123,138-140
  discerning 142
approachability of God 37-40
atonement 31,32
audience with God 18-20,23-31
Augustine 67,86

babbling in prayer 96,153
bedtime prayers 91,92
Bible reading before prayer 44-47

children, prayers for little 75,76
Clement of Rome 92
communication, prayer as special 58-60
communion of saints 155,156
compassion of God 15,16
confidence and prayer 118-120
conversation with God 41-51
creation 13,16

dead, prayers for the 76
divine favor and prayer 61-64
doubt and prayer 118,119,143
doxology 162,163

effectiveness of prayer 144,145
enemies, praying for 75,130-133
etiquette of prayer 81-93
etiquette and respect 81,82

177

ex corde prayers 96-98

faith and prayer 64-68
father, earthly, described 39
Father-God described 38
forgiveness, prayers for 71,159, 160
frequency of prayer 99-101

God as Father 38
gods, false, praying to 145-148
grace defined 64

handbook on prayer 149-163
hands in prayer 88-90
head in prayer 90,91
help, praying for 71,128,129, 161,162
High Priestly Prayer 73,161
Holy Spirit, requesting the 70,136
Holy Spirit helps believers pray 76-79

illness, prayer in time of 73
immortality of God 13

joint prayer 101
judgment, prayer for 130-133
justice of God 14-16
justification 32,66-68

kingdom, praying for God's to come 157
kingdom of God 8,9
kingdom of heaven 8,9

kingship of God 11-16
kneeling in prayer 83-85

language of prayer 95-98,113, 114,117,118
location for prayer 101-105
Lockyer, Herbert 53
Lord's Prayer 97,100,121,135, 149-163
    Fifth Petition 64
    Sixth Petition 50
lordship of God 12,17
Luther and prayer 74,77,78, 96,116,117,120,140,141, 155
lying down in prayer 87,88

material things, prayers for 158,159
mediator, Jesus as 34,35
mercy, praying for 60-64,127, 143,144
misconceptions about prayer 51
model prayer 154,155
Montgomery, James 54
most-favored status 33
motive for prayer 102,103

name of Jesus and prayer 113-118
Newton, John 112
nighttime prayers 91,92
nonverbal communication 54

omnipotence of God 116-120
others, praying for 71-76,129, 130
Our Father. *See* Lord's Prayer

pagans and prayer 96
pattern for prayer 154,155
persecutors, praying for 75,130
persistence in prayer 120-123
person of Trinity addressed in prayer 150-153
persona non grata 20,21,25,26, 33
petitions 50,64,125-136
posture in prayer 82-88
power of God 13-16
praise and adoration in prayer 126,127
prayer, aloud or in the heart 98,99
prayer, continual 99-101
prayer, improper 143
prayer, personal 101-105
prayer books 96-98
prayer unheard by God 23-27, 31
prayer word study 59
prayer-worship 55-58
praying to other gods 145-148
privilege of prayer 42
purposes of God and prayer 142,143

rebels 19-32
reconciliation 27-32

relationships
   between people and God 8
   between subjects and kings 18
   no buddy-buddy relationship with God 38
repentance 33,34
requests denied 141,142
respect owed God 42
responding to God 53,54
right to pray 36
   Jesus alone has 29,30
Roseveare, Dr. Helen 113

sacrifice of Jesus 35
saints, praying to 145-148
sanctification 100,101
self, prayer for 69-71,129,130
sin as barrier 21-25
sitting in prayer 87
standing in prayer 85,86
status in God's kingdom 17-26
survey results 133-136,151

temple, layout as picture of prayer 66
temptation, prayer for aid against 49,70,71,160,161
Tertullian 86,92
thanks in prayer 127,128
triune God addressed in prayer 150-153

unbelievers and prayer 64-68, 143,144

virgin Mary, prayers to 145-148
vocabulary for prayer 95-98, 113,114,117,118

way to God's throne 36
weaknesses in prayer 77,78

will of God and prayer 109-111,157,158
Word of God 43-51,65,79
and prayer 45
word study 60
worship and prayer 54
worship, public 101